Esquire Eats

Esquire Eats

How to Feed Your Friends and Lovers

A MANUAL FOR MEN *by*

FRANCINE MAROUKIAN

FOREWORD *by* DAVID GRANGER

PROJECT EDITOR: BONNIE SLOTNICK
DESIGNER: ELIZABETH VAN ITALLIE
ILLUSTRATOR: K.C. WITHERELL

Library of Congress Cataloging-in-Publication Data
Maroukian, Francine.
    Esquire eats : how to feed your friends and lovers / by Francine Maroukian ; foreword by David Granger.
        p. cm.
Includes index.
    ISBN 1-58816-243-5
1. Dinners and dining. 2. Entertaining. I. Title.
TX737.M376 2004
642'. 4—dc22   2003021001

10   9   8   7   6   5   4   3   2   1

Published by Hearst Books
A Division of Sterling Publishing Co., Inc.
387 Park Avenue South, New York, NY 10016

Esquire is a trademark owned by Hearst Magazines Property, Inc., in USA, and Hearst Communications, Inc., in Canada. Hearst Books is a trademark owned by Hearst Communications, Inc.

www.esquire.com

Distributed in Canada by Sterling Publishing
c/o Canadian Manda Group, One Atlantic Avenue, Suite 105
Toronto, Ontario, Canada M6K 3E7

Distributed in Australia by Capricorn Link (Australia) Pty. Ltd.
P.O. Box 704, Windsor, NSW 2756 Australia

Printed in China

ISBN 1-58816-243-5

Contents

How to Live a Skewer-Free Life

"No, you may not. It will spoil your appetite." Remember that old parental edict? It's still true. The best pre-dinner snacks remain tiny, salty, crisp, and cheesy, and best eaten out of hand.

Meals for Two or Two Couples

Entertaining one other person in your home is a challenge because the host (that's you) is in charge of everything, from conversation to cooking. And since seduction is often the motivation behind dinner for two, the food you serve should possess aphrodisiacal qualities. Unfortunately, cooking inevitably creates chaos, and keeping romance alive in the face of such domesticities as kitchen timing and dirty dishes is tricky business. These menus are designed to limit the number of times you have to excuse yourself and bang around in a messy kitchen. Or, they require only theatrical last-minute cooking that can be performed while the lucky guest watches admiringly.

Once you and your favorite dinner guest manage to become *deux*, this section will assist you in cooking for another couple: Now you've got your compatible foursome, the cornerstone of home entertaining.

Menus for Six to Eight

Entertaining by the numbers: More than four guests means that two conversations can take place at the same time. And both of them without you. Once that happens, it's a party. Our menus are planned around dishes that everyone can enjoy (easy on the exotica), that fit the formality of the occasion, and that are easy to handle (no bones at buffets). The recipes also double easily for larger gatherings.

Recipes for Any Occasion

It isn't always the blockbuster movie that holds our attention; sometimes an independent film is all it takes to entertain us, and the same is true of food. Here are some low-key recipes for dishes that can take you and a few of your friends from a leisurely lunch on a summer weekend to a wintertime Sunday supper without making a huge deal out of it.

Desserts

Programmed by pastry chefs, most people think of dessert as a tower of sweets. But glitzy desserts are restaurant money-makers, more about merchandising than food. Homemade desserts should be simple: simple to make, simple to serve, and above all, simple to eat.

Foreword

Should a woman be writing a cookbook for men?

It's a fair question. Let me answer it by quoting from Francine Maroukian's work for *Esquire*:

"There is no such thing as bad bacon."

"Your typical eleven-hundred-pound steer yields a seven-hundred-pound carcass, and that's a little too much meat at one time for anyone, even me."

And my favorite:

"My entire food philosophy can be summed up with the phrase 'sizzle platter.'"

That's not just a sentence; it's a manifesto.

For the past five years, I've been proud to publish Francine's inimitable food stories (and her fantastic recipes) in the magazine. Every one of them stems from the same basic belief system: The only recipes you need to know are simple, flavorful, and not terribly hard to make. The second part of her belief system is that meals are better when they're cooked at home, for friends.

Esquire Eats is guided by the same idea. This is a manual for men, a kitchen playbook designed to help you plan and execute fantastic meals for two or twelve, all without breaking a sweat. Yes, the recipes are crowd-pleasers. But what sets *Esquire Eats* apart—what makes this book so valuable to any man who enjoys cooking and entertaining at home, by himself or with a significant other—is the freshness of Francine's advice. Drawing from her endless supply of personal anecdotes (the result of twenty years' experience as a professional caterer and a lifetime of feeding her friends), Francine offers truly useful information on how to plan, prep, cook, and even shop for the best ingredients. I mean, would *you* know how to select the best scallops?

I'll leave you with a quick Francine story of my own. In October 2002, we published an article called "How to Eat the Whole Damn Cow," a collection of recipes making use of the entire animal, from the noble porterhouse to the lowly chuck section. The story was vintage Francine: funny, inspired, and above all, useful. It made me hungry, and I did something about it. (Her smoky-chili recipe, which calls for beef *and* bacon, has become one of my favorites; it appears on page 84.) A few days after that issue came out, Francine called to tell me she'd received an invitation to speak at a meeting of the Red Meat Club, a group of Philadelphia carnivores. She was ecstatic. "David!" she practically screamed, "I can't wait: a room full of men and all the red meat I can eat!"

Eat well. Francine won't have it any other way.

—David Granger
Editor in Chief, *Esquire*

Introduction

There are two reasons I have spent most of the last twenty years in a kitchen: I did it for love, and I did it for money.

Although I pulled off some big parties in my catering days (like a sit-down dinner for 350 in the rotunda of the Guggenheim, with Luciano Pavarotti as the guest of honor), the success of those splashy special events rested on my organizational skills and grace-under-pressure personality rather than on the food being served. My menu-planning ability and cooking skills were more evident (and more appreciated) at the home dinner party.

First and foremost, I was a private "carriage trade" caterer with a very small group of clients, primarily on the Upper East Side of Manhattan. My clients had plenty of means, but for the most part, they did not appear to be bound up by their privilege and possessions; they seemed liberated to me. They had been everywhere, so they felt free to entertain at home; they could afford anything they wanted, but preferred to keep it simple. For Julia Child's eighty-sixth birthday dinner, Pamela Fiori, *Town & Country* editor-in-chief, asked me to make a homey *boeuf bourguignonne*. On another occasion, when sixty people paid twenty-five thousand dollars each to have dinner with Vice President Al Gore, that hostess asked me to create an unfussy buffet, centered around grilled honey-and-herb-marinated boneless chicken breasts.

My clients and their confidence about "keeping it small" changed my ideas about entertaining (and, at the risk of sounding affected, changed me as well). In their homes, I learned valuable lessons: that artless doesn't mean careless; that mix doesn't necessarily have to match—and just how expensive "simple" can be. I took these lessons to heart in my own life, using some of my clients' favorite dishes as a way to seduce men and please my friends.

One night, a self-consciously stylish magazine editor came to dinner as the guest of a visiting Australian cult vintner. It was late October, just beginning to get cold at night, and I settled on a menu of wild mushroom lasagna with grilled sausages on the side (for meat-eaters like me), and vanilla ice cream with homemade fudge sauce and peanut butter cookies for dessert (versions of the same meal were probably being served all over America that same night). When the food editor finished eating and asked me (with great seriousness), "How did you think of this?" I was able to pass along what I had learned from my clients about planning menus:

Always choose "crowd pleasers," because if the food you're serving doesn't do that, why bother?

There's another good reason to keep dinner-party cooking low key: Basic recipes will require only basic equipment in kitchens that may fall short of home-magazine design. Entertaining at home can be tough in city apartments, where kitchens are sometimes an afterthought. Even some of my ritzy regular clients, like the late fashion designer Perry Ellis, had kitchen problems. After hauling twenty racks of lamb into his new West Side townhouse for its inaugural dinner party, I discovered that while the professional-grade stainless-steel oven had been installed (as Mr. Ellis had assured me), the glass had not been fitted into the oven door, rendering it useless. I ended up "borrowing" the kitchen of The Silver Palate, a famous take-out food shop only a few blocks away. My crew and I timed the meal by telephone, running down Columbus Avenue with trays bearing sizzling racks of lamb when it was time to serve the main course.

I doubt you will encounter anything so dramatic in your home, but if I managed to make these meals in the many troubled kitchens I encountered (including my own, which I swear was once a coat closet), so can you—no matter where you live.

As you read through this book, you might think the menus I've put together are too plain to be "special" enough for entertaining. Well, you can make fancier, fussier food if you want to: You can roast beets and then peel them until your fingers are pink-tipped; create savory infusions that you start hours ahead of time with a pile of veal bones; you can even change the everyday into the exotic by incorporating strange ingredients, like lasagna made with layers of squid-ink noodles and truffles, if it makes you happy. It's just not necessary in order to make your guests happy. There's no reason to bowl people over with food, even on special occasions.

The most sophisticated palates appreciate simple food when it is prepared well, and there will always be a certain assurance in serving classic dishes. Besides, we're not trying to make history here, just dinner.

How to Use This Book

As a devotee of the fabulously addictive television drama *Law & Order,* I consider myself to be just a few episodes away from a law degree. But television—even great television—won't turn me into an attorney. The same is true for cooking shows and lifestyle programs: You will never learn to be a good host unless you actually get up off the couch and try.

The menu game plans in this book are designed to step-by-step you through many entertaining evenings. Although you are not going to find *ooh-la-la* celebrity chef food, be forewarned: You won't find any broccoli or cauliflower recipes either. These menus may be simple, but they are not intended to feed families or save money. Yes, anyone can fold these dishes into their recipe repertoire. But first and foremost, this is a book of strategies for entertaining—entertaining adults. Along with each menu are tips to help you understand the hows and whys of entertaining. Watch for the following markers.

Social Scenario: What goes with whom

Serving the right food to the right people is part of good party planning. Some of our menus are designed to be prepared in advance, leaving you with just a few finishing touches to accomplish while guests are present— perfect for those times when you want to focus on the people rather than the food. Other menus are more challenging—excellent meals to make for old friends, guests who don't mind when you disappear into the kitchen (or those who can be trusted to accompany you and stay out of the way).

Stacking Textures: What goes with what

When it comes to fashion, appreciating the power of a good suit is one thing; knowing how to accessorize it is another. The same is true for food. Big deal: You've decided to serve a porterhouse. But a porterhouse with what?

Partnering a main course with the right sides takes practice, and it helps to understand the menu *ménage à trois:* crisp, crunchy, creamy. When it comes to balancing a plate, color and flavor are important elements, but texture is essential. For example, a menu that starts with carrot and ginger soup, followed by fillet of beef, wild rice and sautéed spinach, topped off with lemon mousse for dessert, can make you a little dizzy and kind of bored, anxious for it all to be over. That meal will feel interminable because it is too consistently thick and rich: You need a little snap and crunch.

Consider the same fillet preceded by a soup of slivered watercress floating in beef broth and paired with crisp potatoes and lemon-pepper green beans, followed by pecan tartlets for dessert. That menu works better because it is not repetitive; it has contrasting flavors, colors and textures. (When party food is served buffet style, side-by-side pairings aren't as critical, since guests usually assemble their own plates and don't think about texture; they just take what they like.)

Cooking Strategy: When and where to cook it

Achieving a perfect plate has as much to do with timing as with taste. In addition to balancing flavors and textures, you want to coordinate cooking methods in order to avoid kitchen snarl-ups—like trying to roast two things at different temperatures in the same oven at the same time.

The Equipment

It may be hard to believe, but there are times when the success of a dish depends more on the equipment than the ingredients. We'll point out exactly what you need to get the best out of a recipe.

Giving Good Host

For many people, a constant diet of restaurant meals has become the norm, and entertaining at home the rare treat. But even years of expense-account eating won't teach you the truth about home entertaining—perfection isn't as important as personality. Here are little secrets to help inspire casual confidence, dispelling that invisible but party-killing air of trying too hard. We understand that there are plenty of books and magazines with gorgeous food styling and flawless photography to show you how good a party can *look*. We will have done our job when you understand how good a party can *feel*.

Use Everything

When there are serving or leftover options, we'll tell you.

The Skills

When a recipe will benefit from a certain technique, we'll help you master it.

How to Buy

When a little more information will make your shopping easier, we'll make sure you have it.

The Best

When there really is a difference in ingredients, we'll let you know.

Esquire Eats

Starters

1

Starters
Or, How To Live a Skewer-Free Life

There may be racks and racks of cooking and lifestyle magazines, but it still falls to *Esquire* to deliver the news: There is such a thing as *too much food*. And there is definitely such a thing as too much food before dinner.

Overfeeding usually occurs in the home of nervous (or new) hosts, mostly because they confuse those ornate hors d'oeuvre served at cocktail parties in lieu of dinner with the little teasers meant to enhance a guest's appetite *before* dinner. Think of the times you've waited for a table in the best restaurant bars: Did anyone offer you a cube of chicken impaled on a flimsy bamboo skewer with some drippy sauce? No, they didn't. They tendered bite-size snacks (like olives and salted nuts) that kept your hand straying back to the bowl over and over again. That's exactly what you want to serve before dinner in your home: something to occupy your guests while you are putting the final touches on dinner, and to introduce the idea that the real meal is on the way.

The Three Commandments:

(1) Just so you know, *hors d'oeuvre,* meaning "outside (or before) the meal," is never written in the plural form. No matter the variety of hors d'oeuvre served or quantity eaten, there is only one meal, so there's no such thing as "hors d'oeuvres."

(2) Never use the term "finger foods" unless you are Hannibal Lecter.

(3) No matter what sort of lactose-intolerant, gluten-free fitness freak you might be, serving a carrot stick (or any raw vegetable) with a cocktail is a vulgar practice that puts the crude in crudités. Fortunately, the tiny, salty, crispy, cheesy tidbits that make the best and easiest starters are not hard to find. The two standard-bearers are olives and nuts.

All About Olives

Olives may be the perfect appetite enhancer, and taking time to scout out good ones from a fancy food market (many of which have "olive bars" for sampling) or ethnic grocery is well worth the trouble. You'll find two basic varieties: green and black, with varying shades in between. With that information out of the way, we'll let Ari Weinzweig, olive expert and CEO of Zingerman's in Ann Arbor, Michigan (a "deli" that's a Mecca for food insiders), explain the rest.

"The color of an olive mostly indicates the degree of ripeness at which it was picked. As with many other types of fruit, green olives are not ripe and usually have a firm, almost crisp texture (again, think of the texture of any unripe fruit) and a nutty flavor.

"Black olives, on the other hand, have been allowed to remain on the tree until they're fully ripe. As with other ripe fruit, the added maturing means they will be softer in texture, sweeter and richer in flavor. In truth, though, what we often refer to as 'black' really runs the gamut from light brown to beautiful shades of red and purple, all the way down to the deepest, darkest, most devilish black. It is also true that different olive varieties do have different 'typical' colors. Some are darker, some lighter; some browner, some more of a purplish-black."

As for Ari's thoughts on canned California black olives (i.e., why they are still sold), many folks have fond memories of sticking the pitted olives on the ends of their fingers, which in his judgment is probably their best—or maybe their only—use.

HOW TO BUY OLIVES

Alfonsos: Grown along the northern and western coasts of South America. Alfonsos are still unusual in this country, but they're destined to be more and more popular in the coming years. Large, meaty purple olives with a unique fruity flavor, they make distinctive additions to party platters.

Amfissa: Soft-textured purple-black Greek olives from the area around Delphi, the legendary home of the Greek oracles. (If you eat enough of them you may be able to predict the future.)

Cerignola: Huge (the size of a shell-on walnut), crisp green olives from the area around Bari in the province of Puglia down in Italy's southeast corner. They make impressive additions to antipasto platters. Beware of the many Cerignola olives on the market which are dyed green. There are also black Cerignolas being sold which are cured much like the canned California olives (see opposite page), but they are of much better quality.

Gaeta: Purple-brown olives from central Italy. Good in pasta dishes or on pizzas (nearby Naples is the home of the pizza).

Gordal: *Gorda* means "fat" in Spanish, and it's an appropriate name for these large green olives. They have a firm, meaty texture and ben-

efit from the addition of southern Spanish seasonings such as cumin, garlic, thyme, and a splash of sherry vinegar.

Hondroelia: The biggest olives I've ever eaten, in both size and flavor. Almost two inches long, they're so substantial you eat them with a knife and fork (though I confess to using my hands and eating them more like a peach or a plum); the Greeks refer to them as "olives for heroes." Hard to find but delicious.

Kalamata: The best known of the Greek olives, Kalamatas come from the valley of Messina on the western end of the Peloponnesian peninsula, near the town of Kalamata. They have a distinctive, pointed almond shape and a beautiful black-purple color. The flavor of Kalamatas is made even more distinctive because of their curing—they're cracked and then cured in a red wine vinegar brine that gives them an almost wine-like flavor. Without question, the best Kalamatas I've ever had were hand-picked. There's a night and day difference between the silky smooth, rich texture of the best hand-picked product and the barrels full of inexpensive, slightly bitter, oft-bruised Kalamatas that are commonly available in every deli. There are huge differences in Kalamata quality on the market, so you really need to taste and com-

pare before you settle on a source.

Ligurian: Black olives of the Italian Riviera with a sweet, delicate flavor. I like to marinate them with a bit of orange peel, fennel, fresh garlic cloves, and olive oil (from Liguria, of course).

Manzanilla: Smaller, crisper, and nuttier than Gordal, these cracked, brownish-green olives are some of Spain's best. The name means "little apple," a reference to their round shape. Try them dressed with olive oil and a generous dose of chopped fresh garlic.

Mission: The most widely grown California olive. Originally planted to be processed and canned, although some are picked early and pressed for oil. Fortunately, some are dry-cured for eating; these olives are wrinkled and shiny-skinned, with a slightly bitter flavor.

Moroccan: The olive markets of Morocco are an impressive sight, with mounds of multi-colored olives dressed with an array of different spices. The most readily available in this country are the dry-cured black Moroccan olives, which have a meaty texture akin to dried prunes and are excellent when marinated with North African seasonings such as cumin and hot chilies.

Nafplion: Cracked green olives from Greece with a nutty, slightly smoky flavor that's enhanced by dressing them with lemon juice and fresh dill.

Niçoise: These tiny black jewels of the olive world, with their uniquely delicate flavor, come from the south of France. Essential in authentic Provençal dishes such as salade niçoise or pissaladière, an onion, olive, and anchovy "pizza." I love these olives.

Nyons: Some of the best olives around, and another of my favorites, French Nyons are plump and politely wrinkled, with large smooth pits. They're particularly good dressed with Provençal olive oil and wild herbs like thyme and rosemary.

Picholine: Crisp, uncracked green olives from southern France, Picholines have a nice nutty flavor with anise undertones. Try them with fresh fennel and olive oil.

Thasos: Also known as Throumbes, these shriveled, wrinkled olives come from the Greek island of Thasos. They have a nice meaty texture and an intensely olivey flavor. Try them dressed with a little olive oil and oregano.

Sevillano: Large, meaty, brine-cured green California olives, similar to the Spanish-style. Gordals.

Nuts

Don't settle for any nut selection called a "party mix." People will just paw through and pick out the cashews anyway. Focus on a single kind of nut (shelled, of course), such as roasted Spanish almonds with sea salt (roasting intensifies the flavor), or a "treated" nut in a mild but intriguing flavor, such as sugared/cumin pecans. Nutshells are a natural defense against heat, light, and moisture, but shelled nuts spoil quickly. (Fresh nuts are crisp; they'll break rather than bend.) It's best to buy nuts packaged in a vacuum-sealed jar or can. If you shop at a store that sells in bulk from bins, get small quantities, and only at a shop with a rapid turnover (lots of customers; very little dust). Store the nuts in an airtight container in the refrigerator or freezer.

Tapas From Takeout

With all the offerings from fancy food markets and specialty stores, you can put together a robust selection of starters in the style of Spanish tapas (a variety of appetizers typically served with sherry or cocktails), Italian antipasto (appetizers served "before the meal"), or an All-American "trip around the kitchen." From grilled mini-artichoke hearts and tiny hot peppers stuffed with prosciutto to herb-flavored popcorn and crunchy cheese straws, you don't actually have to make anything yourself (unless you want to). Your only job is to make what you've bought look good.

Whether you are setting out only one or an assortment of starters, small is better (really and truly). Keep the portions modest and the plates pared down. Instead of using oversized platters and trays for large gatherings (they're hard to keep attractive and take too long to refill), make duplicate sets of starters and put the food where you want the people to go. When it comes to starters that require assembly (like a savory spread served on toasted bread), many people are reluctant to be the first to dig in. Help your guests to help themselves by offering several prearranged toasts, urging people to refill at will.

GIVING GOOD HOST: STYLING STARTERS

Save the Southwestern pottery for your next barbecue and hide those silly bar theme doodads; the right look for cocktail starters is metro-modern. Take a minimalist approach and work with the sleek, clean lines of shallow porcelain (or china) plates and bowls to keep your offerings looking crisp and sculptural. Choose varying shapes and sizes in the same color family for a rich tone-on-tone contemporary look; this will create a unifying thread between the dishes regardless of their silhouette. You can go to extremes with black or white, or select from a neutral palette such as cool grays and celadon green, letting the food provide the color. Other possibilities include a relish or tapas tray (a modular set of dishes that fit on a tray to form "compartments") and olive boats, narrow canoe-shaped servers designed to hold olives (or nuts) in a single row rather than piled in a deep bowl.

Dips and Spreads

Perhaps these savory spreads bear little resemblance to the onion dip of your potato chip-intensive childhood, but they are just as addictive. Save yourself some time by making them in advance.

GREEN OLIVE AND WALNUT TAPENADE

Use a soft, meaty olive like the brownish-green Atalanta, or any fleshy green olive. You can chop the olives in a small food processor fitted with a metal blade as long as you don't pulverize them. However, hand-grating the cheese is a must; it will give the tapenade a rougher, more interesting texture.

5 tablespoons walnut oil
⅓ cup walnut pieces
3 cloves garlic, finely chopped
¾ cup green olives, pitted and finely chopped
About ⅓ cup finely chopped flat-leaf parsley
1 teaspoon ground black pepper
pinch of red pepper flakes
⅓ cup hand-grated Parmigiano-Reggiano

1. In a medium skillet over low heat, gently warm 2 tablespoons of the oil. Add the walnuts and toss to coat. Cook, stirring frequently, until the nuts are golden, 3 to 5 minutes. Add the garlic and cook, stirring frequently, until lightly colored and fragrant, 2 minutes. While this mixture is still warm, transfer it to the bowl of a small food processor and pulse until it resembles a thick paste. Let cool.

2. In a small bowl, combine the olives, parsley, black and red pepper, and remaining 3 tablespoons of oil. Fold in the ground walnut mixture and the grated cheese and let stand at room temperature for at least an hour. Add more black and/or red pepper to taste, and serve with toasted country bread.

MAKES ABOUT 3 CUPS

USE EVERYTHING
To serve leftover tapenade as a pasta sauce: Moisten drained hot pasta with some of the pasta cooking water—about 1 tablespoon per serving—and toss with tapenade, like pesto.
To use leftover ricotta dip the same way, add the cheese mixture to the hot, moistened pasta little by little, tossing until coated.

RICOTTA WITH PROSCIUTTO AND BASIL

This creamy spread is studded with crisp sautéed prosciutto that highlights the mild sweetness of the ricotta.

1½ lb. ricotta cheese, drained of excess liquid
2 tablespoons olive oil
4 cloves garlic, finely chopped
¼ lb. sliced prosciutto, cut into ¼-inch dice
⅓ cup basil leaves, torn into tiny pieces
2 teaspoons ground black pepper

1. Place the ricotta in a mixing bowl. In a heavy medium skillet, heat the oil over medium heat. Add the garlic and cook, stirring frequently, until fragrant and golden, 2 to 3 minutes. Add the prosciutto and stir until it begins to change color, 2 to 3 minutes longer. Scrape the prosciutto and garlic into the bowl of ricotta and mix well. Refrigerate if not serving immediately.

2. Before serving, bring the spread to room temperature and fold in the basil and pepper. Serve with toasted country bread.

MAKES ABOUT 3 CUPS

TONNATO

Thicker than the tuna sauce served with veal in the classic vitello tonnato, this earthy spread can also be used as a dip for shrimp.

3 tablespoons capers, drained and rinsed
2 tablespoons balsamic vinegar
2 (6-ounce) cans Italian tuna (packed in olive oil), drained
1 tablespoon olive oil
2 teaspoons mayonnaise
1 tablespoon finely chopped flat-leaf parsley
½ teaspoon ground black pepper

Soak the capers in vinegar for about 15 minutes. Place the tuna and olive oil in the bowl of a small food processor and pulse to combine. Add the capers and vinegar; process to a thick paste. Transfer to a small bowl and fold in the mayonnaise. Add the parsley and pepper and stir to combine. Serve with toasted country bread.

MAKES ABOUT 2 CUPS

Under it All: the Bread

Crumbly storebought crackers cannot compare to homemade crostini or bruschetta in flavor, texture or sturdiness.

CROSTINI

These thin, crisp cocktail-size toasts are perfect for spreads and dips. They are just big enough to be consumed in one or two bites with something salty or cheesy on top.

Cut a baguette (quality is everything) into ¼-inch slices (cut on the diagonal so there will be more spreading surface). Brush both sides with olive oil and lay the slices on a sheet pan. Toast in a preheated 375°F oven for 3 to 5 minutes, or until lightly browned on the surface but not hard all the way through (the timing depends on the bread you use).

BRUSCHETTA

Larger bruschetta-style toasts are meant to be topped with heartier offerings like roasted or marinated vegetables and served like open-faced sandwiches. They are easy to make as long as you start with a crusty country loaf purchased from a good bakery (quality is everything).

Cut the bread into thick slices (about ⅓ inch); whether you leave the slices whole or cut them in half depends on the shape of the loaf. Place the sliced bread directly on the rack of a preheated 375°F oven (no pan required) until crisp on the surface but not hard all the way through (the timing depends on the bread you use).

THE EQUIPMENT: TOAST RACK
When serving toasted bread as an accompaniment, avoid the rustic wicker basket trap by using a toast rack. A onetime staple of upper-crust English life, toast racks (like letter holders, with a central handle and vertical separators) come in silver or silverplate; more contemporary models may be chrome or stainless. Antique racks—good flea-market finds—are often sold in pairs. You can also lay the bread out on a flat plate (easy to pick up), or "file" the toasts in a deep, narrow bowl.

Slow-Roasted Tomatoes

Spread a slice of toasted baguette with a flavorful soft cheese, such as *gorgonzola dolce* or tangy peppercorn chèvre, and top with these rich, intensely flavorful tomatoes. The plum tomato halves are perfectly sized to fit atop and transform the predictable bread-and-cheese combination into something luscious.

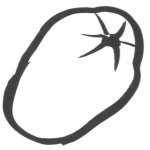

SLOW-ROASTED TOMATOES

Use cooking parchment (see page 30) rather than foil to prevent the tomatoes from sticking to the pan. It's specially prepared to withstand high temperatures, and is available at any kitchen supply store.

6 ripe Roma (plum) tomatoes, about ¾ pound
Olive oil
Coarse or kosher salt and ground black pepper

1. Preheat the oven to 325°F. Line a large heavy-gauge sheet pan with cooking parchment.

2. Halve the tomatoes lengthwise. Scoop out and discard the pulp and seeds, then blot the excess liquid from the tomatoes with paper towels. Toss the tomatoes with the oil (they should be coated but not drenched), then place them cut-side up in the pan and sprinkle with salt and pepper.

3. Roast the tomatoes until they dry out and begin to shrivel but are still slightly wet in the middle, about 90 minutes (cooking time depends on the ripeness and size of the tomatoes). Turn off the heat but leave the tomatoes in the oven to finish cooking as the oven cools, about another 25 minutes. Remove the pan from the oven and let the tomatoes cool in the pan on a rack.

MAKES 12

The Cheese Straw, Wafer, or Penny

I always wondered why crisp little cheese pastries—straws, wafers, or "pennies"—are such a staple of the Southern party sideboard. Then I asked John Martin Taylor, a Southern culinary historian known as Hoppin' John. "Well, it seems to me that, at one time, it was the best way to 'preserve' cheese in the hot and humid South. But they remain popular these days because we Southerners have that whole nostalgic thing about the food our mothers and grandmothers made. Plus, they're good, and most important, good with drinks. And drink we do. How can you not in this God-awful heat?"

Although most fancy food markets stock a shelf full of serviceable cheese crackers, these pepper-spiked Cheddar shortbreads, especially good with drinks, are easy enough to make a specialty of your house.

THE EQUIPMENT: SILICONE BAKING MAT
Just the greatest thing to come out of France, a flexible, heatproof (up to 500°F) baking-pan liner that keeps the bottom surface of foods (such as these shortbreads or other cookies) from burning or sticking to the pan. (The French "Silpat" is the original and most popular brand.) You can substitute cooking parchment, a greaseproof paper that won't flame, specially made for kitchen use.

CHEDDAR CHEESE SHORTBREAD

This recipe came to me through Jan Fort, a food stylist I met when I was catering. Like most good Southern girls, she inherited the recipe from her mother. Mrs. Fort's recipe was meant to produce thin, fragile wafers, formed with a cookie press. Because I over-beat the dough and then, lacking the patience to maneuver a cookie press, used my hands to shape it, I ended up with thick, cheesy shortbread medallions. For this recipe, the butter needs to sit at room temperature until it is pliable but not yet soft. Unwrap the butter and cut it in pieces while it is still cold, then set it out to soften slightly.

8 ounces extra-sharp orange Cheddar cheese, shredded (2 cups)
1½ sticks (¾ cup) unsalted butter, cut into small pieces
2 cups unbleached all-purpose flour
½ teaspoon cayenne pepper
¼ teaspoon ground black pepper

1. Preheat the oven to 375°F. Line a heavy-gauge sheet pan with cooking parchment or a Silpat mat.

2. In a large bowl, using an electric mixer, cream the cheese and butter at medium speed until well combined (it will look a little like lumpy orange paste). Stir together the flour, cayenne, and black pepper. Add this mixture to the cheese mixture about ½ cup at a time, beating at high speed and stopping to scrape down the sides, until the mixture pulls away from the sides of the bowl and forms a ball.

3. Gently roll small hunks of dough between the flattened palms of your hands, shaping the dough into walnut-size balls. Place the dough balls on the prepared pan, at least 2 inches apart. Using the back of a fork, press the tines down to gently flatten each ball. Bake until the bottom of the shortbread is browned and the top is set, about 14 minutes. The inside of the shortbread will still be slightly soft. Transfer the shortbreads to a rack to cool.

MAKES 24

Shrimp Two Ways

For a former caterer like me, shrimp is divided into two categories: stand-up or skewered shrimp (a/k/a "sputnik" shrimp, because of the way a round silver tray with skewers sticking over the edge looks), and sit-down shrimp (rarely a main course, but occasionally served as a restaurant-style first course). As someone who catered several parties a week for about fifteen years, I have personally peeled more shrimp than most people will ever see in their lives.

Although (believe it or not) I still love shrimp, these days I don't eat anything standing up. I like to eat my shrimp sitting down, particularly in these two versions: crisp, classic shrimp cocktail, and a rosemary-infused variation on scampi. Although both can be eaten out of hand (no one ever complains that shrimp are too messy to pick up), you can also provide small (cocktail-size) plates: no forks required.

HOW TO BUY SHRIMP

Buying shrimp is a serious job; don't even think about cutting corners. Freshness, even in frozen shrimp, is of paramount importance. Almost all shrimp being sold has been frozen. But when it's been frozen for too long (or improperly), the taste and texture suffer. Shrimp that have not been handled correctly can become soggy and mineral-y, like cotton balls soaked in iodine-infused water.

Buying "fresh" shrimp (thawed in the store) from a reputable fish market is always first choice. But when the only option is frozen, boxed supermarket shrimp, check the package carefully to make sure there is no leakage or surface ice (which can mean that the box has been defrosted and refrozen).

Shrimp are sold according to size, and although specifications vary slightly from region to region, buy "large" or "21–25" shrimp (meaning there are between twenty-one and twenty-five shrimp in a pound). Refrigerate the shrimp in a plastic bag placed over ice until ready to use, peeling and cleaning them as close to cooking time as possible.

SHRIMP COCKTAIL

A good shrimp cocktail should have the layered, complex flavors of an herb-and-spice-infused cooking liquid and the sweet heat of a tomato-based dipping sauce laced with horseradish. It should also have just the right temperature and texture: chilled, but without the metallic tang of the refrigerator; cold, but not hard. The best way to achieve this is to plunge the shrimp into an ice bath right after cooking them. Many restaurants serve them that way, as well—a few delicately manicured shrimp arrayed on crushed ice.

3 bay leaves
1 teaspoon whole black peppercorns
1 tablespoon plus 1 teaspoon whole cloves
1 tablespoon plus 1 teaspoon whole allspice
1 tablespoon plus 1 teaspoon whole mustard seeds
¼ teaspoon red pepper flakes
1 lb. large (21–25 count) unpeeled shrimp

1. Combine the herbs and spices in a muslin spice bag (available at any kitchen supply store). Use one spice bag for each pound of shrimp.

2. Place the spice bag and 6 quarts of water in a medium stockpot (at least 8 quarts). Bring the water to a rapid boil over high heat. Lower the heat slightly but continue boiling for at least 5 minutes to infuse the water with herbs and spices (you will smell them). Meanwhile, make an ice bath by placing 3 trays of ice cubes and 3 cups of cold water in a large mixing bowl.

3. Add the shrimp to the boiling water and cook until just tender and still slightly translucent in the center, about 3 minutes. Using a slotted spoon, remove the shrimp and immediately plunge them into the ice bath. When the shrimp are cool, drain and peel them.

SERVES 4 AS AN APPETIZER

COCKTAIL SAUCE

Serve the sauce in small portions, keeping back-up containers in the refrigerator so the sauce is always fresh and cold. Small (about 2-ounce) white porcelain ramekins (like miniature soufflé dishes) will work. They are often sold in multi-packs at kitchen supply stores and are also useful for individual servings of jam, syrup, or salt.

12-ounce jar Heinz chili sauce
3 tablespoons grated white horseradish (or more if you are stout-hearted),
   available in refrigerated jars at the supermarket
2 tablespoons Worcestershire sauce

Combine all the ingredients in a small mixing bowl. Refrigerate the sauce until ready to use and serve cold, cold cold.

MAKES ABOUT 1½ CUPS (AND KEEPS WELL IN THE REFRIGERATOR)

THE SKILLS: HOW TO PEEL SHRIMP

Using small, short-bladed kitchen scissors (often sold with Asian cooking supplies), hold the shrimp with the head toward you and cut along the length of the back, exposing the intestinal vein (and, if you're lucky, removing it as well). Peel the shell away; leaving the tail on depends on the nature of the recipe and your own preferences. If the scissors haven't removed the vein, rinse the shrimp under cool, gently running water until cleaned. Drain thoroughly.

SHRIMP WITH ROSEMARY

The key to sautéing shrimp is a hot pan that conducts heat well. Adjust the heat so the surface of the shrimp sears immediately. For a pick-up starter, drain the pan juices and arrange the shrimp in a small plate or shallow bowl. For a plated first course, serve the shrimp alongside a slice of grilled bread, topped with the pan juices.

1 tablespoon unsalted butter
2 tablespoons olive oil
3 cloves garlic, finely chopped
2 shallots, finely chopped
1 lb. large shrimp (21–25 count), peeled and deveined
2 tablespoons fresh lemon juice
2 teaspoons finely chopped flat-leaf parsley
1 teaspoon finely chopped fresh rosemary
Coarse or kosher salt and ground black pepper

1. In a large, heavy skillet over low heat, melt the butter with the oil until foamy. Add the garlic and shallots, cooking only until fragrant and golden brown, about 3 minutes. Adjust the heat to medium-high and add the shrimp. Cook, turning occasionally, until the surface of the shrimp is golden brown but the interior still looks slightly translucent, 3 to 5 minutes.

2. Remove the skillet from the heat and toss the shrimp with the lemon juice, parsley, and rosemary. Season with salt and pepper.

SERVES 4 AS AN APPETIZER

THE EQUIPMENT: HEAVY-GAUGE SHEET PAN
One of the most valuable pieces of kitchen equipment you will ever own is a commercial-weight sheet pan. Also called a jelly-roll pan, this 18 x13-inch heavy-gauge pan (with a 1-inch rolled rim) allows for maximum exposure. You can use this pan for baking cookies or oven-roasting a rack of lamb. High-quality professional bakeware will never warp.

Pour Deux

1 Double-Fired Porterhouse with Classic Steakhouse Rub, Lemon-Peppered Green Beans, Flash Home-Fries

2 Moroccan Lamb Shanks with Orange and Olive Gremolata, Middle Eastern Quesadillas

3 Seafood Risotto, Fennel and Celery Salad

4 Roast Chicken, Skillet Asparagus, Mashed Reds

5 Peppered Tuna, Spinach with Garlic, Popcorn New Potatoes

6 Lamb Kebabs *or* Oven-roasted Lamb Chops *or* Rack of Lamb, Almond-Parsley Pilaf, Romaine and Dill Salad

2

Pour Deux
Meals for Two or Two Couples

1/Double-Fired Porterhouse with Classic Steakhouse Rub
➤ Lemon-Peppered Green Beans
➤ Flash Home-Fries

Although I am embarrassed by it now, I once fell for a fancy man, a man so pale and delicately boned that the first time I saw him stretched out in my bathtub he looked like something that had been filleted. He was the kind of guy who wore silk pajamas, refused to go barefoot, and believed you could have too much sex but never enough seduction.

Since Fancy Man was a boutique wine salesman, we spent most of our nights in expensive restaurants where one glance would have told anyone that we were poorly matched. His plates were always artful tableaux—crisp little birds hovering on pools of brightly colored purées, and cunningly arranged fruit desserts encased in spun-sugar cages—while mine had a childish paint-by-number quality: red meat and green vegetables followed by a little something chocolate. Fancy Man tolerated my indifference toward *haute cuisine* as long as he could, until the evening he reached across the table, tapped the tines of his fork on the edge of my plate, and hissed, "You eat like a gun moll."

It wasn't as bad as it sounds. He meant that I eat passionately, with an appetite that comes out of desire and not from what is fashionable in food. And he was right. We had different engines, this man and I; we needed different fuels to stoke our fires. His constitution could be satisfied by exotic tidbits, while my body craves some-

thing substantial, like steak—or more precisely, steak on the bone.

Since I eat a lot of red meat (and can no longer rely on Fancy Man's fancy expense account to provide it), I have developed a simple technique for making steakhouse-quality steaks at home. I sear the meat on top of the stove in a very hot skillet and finish cooking it in the oven, saving time, mess, and fat-dripping broiler fires.

Stacking Textures

Partnering a main course as rich as red meat with side dishes is a challenge. In Italy, *bistecca alla fiorentina* (the famous grilled beefsteak) is often accompanied by lemon wedges or a cruet of balsamic vinegar—a touch of acidity that serves to pierce the thick creaminess of the meat. In this case, adding lemon zest and lemon juice at the last moment when searing the green beans provides a similar flavor lift. The potatoes used for the flash home-fries are prebaked in a way that produces the perfect ratio of crisp skin to cooked flesh, which quickly absorbs the butter and oil to become extra-crusty— exactly the texture combination you want with red meat. Dessert: any kind of fruit crisp (page 153), served cold (no matter what the season) with whipped cream (plain, or flavored to match the fruit) instead of ice cream.

Social Scenario

Revenge may be a dish best served cold, but these home fries and green beans should go directly from the pan to the plate to the table. While the steak is resting, you'll need to give your full attention to cooking on both burners, making this menu part litmus test, part first home dinner *pour deux*. You'll quickly learn if your guest can't stand the heat.

Cooking Strategy

Searing the steak takes concentration: For a short, intense period, your attention will be consumed by your task because everything is hot at once—the oil, the skillet, the oven. The hot oil keeps the meat from sticking to the pan and helps to form a crust on the exterior of the steak, and the preheated oven will continue the cooking process you jump-started on top of the stove.

THE BEST BEEF

On its way from the meat-packer to the plate, a side of beef is divided into nine sections (called primal or wholesale cuts) before being butchered into standard retail supermarket cuts of meat. (Specific cuts, like our 2½-inch-thick porterhouse, generally come from a butcher and are not available prepackaged in the refrigerated meat case at the grocery store.)

Although the names given each cut may vary from region to region (a very confusing practice that exists mostly for marketing reasons), one thing never changes: Tenderness sets the price. The more money you spend on a cut of beef, the less time it takes to prepare.

1. Expensive These tender steaks can all be dry-cooked (roasted, pan-sautéed, broiled, grilled).

Short loin: porterhouse, T-bone, filet mignon and top loin steak (which is also called a shell, New York or Kansas City strip, club, or ambassador steak, depending on whether there is a bone or not.)

Rib: rib-eye, a boneless steak, sometimes called a Delmonico or spencer steak, and rib steaks, which are cut from the rib roast and have a bone.

2. In the Middle *Sirloin:* This section, closer to the rump, is less tender. But to me, boneless sirloin steak has real flavor and the right kind of chewiness. It is also a good steak to cook for two. Ask the butcher to cut your steak at least 2 inches thick and don't cook it past medium-rare. Slice thickly at an angle to serve.

3. Less money; more work Cuts like chuck, brisket, and flank must be marinated or moist-cooked (braised, pot-roasted or stewed).

THE EQUIPMENT: NONSTICK SKILLET AND TONGS
You will need a heavy-gauge skillet that fits your burner, with a *durable nonstick surface* and *oven-proof handle.* This is not a place to save money. The pan should be heavy enough to conduct heat well—the better the material under the nonstick coating, the better the skillet will work. You'll also need long, sturdy tongs (preferably with a spring lock for easy storage) so you don't pierce the meat when you turn it.

The most experienced cooks just poke the steak with their fingers, knowing that the softer the steak, the less resistance it yields to the touch, the rarer it is. More cautious cooks insert an instant-read meat thermometer into the center of the steak, watching as it registers 115–120°F for rare; 125–130°F for medium-rare. But if you're just starting out in the kitchen, it is acceptable to make a slit in the steak and peek, bearing in mind that the meat will continue to cook (about another 5°F) as it rests.

DOUBLE-FIRED PORTERHOUSE WITH CLASSIC STEAKHOUSE RUB

When you start with good beef, it doesn't take a lot of fussing to make a great steak. Usually, kosher salt and black pepper are all you need. But when you crave a livelier layer of flavor, try a dry rub. Unlike marinades, used to tenderize less expensive (tougher) pieces of meat, dry rubs add flavor to meat that is already tender. Rub the mixture into the steaks and let them sit at room temperature for at least an hour to make sure the spices are absorbed into the meat by the time you are ready to cook. (Even a thin layer of excess rub makes the surface of the cooked steaks a little mushy.)

2 teaspoons ground mustard (not mustard powder)
2 teaspoons granulated garlic
2 teaspoons coarse or kosher salt
1 teaspoon finely ground black pepper
1 porterhouse steak, cut about 2½ inches thick (about 2¾ lb.)
Olive oil
Juice of 1 lemon (optional)

1. Combine the mustard, garlic, salt, and pepper. Coat both sides of the steak with the spice mixture and let the meat sit at room temperature for at least an hour. The longer the steak sits, the stronger the taste of the spice mixture will be.

2. Preheat the oven to 375°F. Lightly film the bottom of an ovenproof nonstick skillet with oil (wiping out the excess with a paper towel) and heat over high heat until the pan is very hot but the oil is not smoking (timing depends on the size of your pan and how well it conducts heat). Using long tongs, carefully place the steak in the pan and sear until a crust forms, turning only once (about 3 minutes on first side, 2 on the flip side).

3. Place the skillet in the oven to finish cooking the steak, 8 to 10 minutes for rare, 10 to 12 for medium-rare.

4. Transfer the steak to a cutting board and let it rest for about 10 minutes to allow the natural juices to redistribute. Using a knife with a thin, sharp blade, cut the meat away from the bone. Carve each portion of meat into thick slices and reassemble around the bone on a serving platter.

5. Optional deglazing: While the steak is resting, place the hot skillet over medium heat and add the lemon juice. Use a wooden spoon to mix the lemon juice with the cooking liquids, letting the mixture bubble up any browned bits that are stuck to the pan. Lower the heat and simmer until the juices are slightly thickened, about 2 minutes. Pour the sauce over the sliced steak and serve.

SERVES 2

LEMON-PEPPERED GREEN BEANS

"Shocking" the beans in ice water as soon as they're done stops the cooking and locks in the bright green color. It ensures that the beans will be crisp and not mushy. In a pinch, I occasionally use precooked green beans from my neighborhood salad bar, but only if they are bright green, firm, and full, right down to the tips.

½ lb. green beans, trimmed
1 tablespoon unsalted butter
1 tablespoon olive oil
1 large shallot, peeled and minced
1 teaspoon minced lemon zest
2 tablespoons fresh lemon juice
Kosher salt and coarsely-ground black pepper

1. Bring an 8-quart stockpot of salted water to a boil. Meanwhile, make an ice bath by placing 2 trays of ice cubes in a large mixing bowl and adding cold water until the bowl is three-quarters full. For an extra boost, place the bowl in the freezer until ready to use.

2. Cook the green beans in the boiling water until crisp-tender, about 2 minutes. (Like pasta, green beans need a lot of room to cook properly.) Using long tongs, quickly transfer the beans to the ice bath. When the beans are completely cooled, drain, pat dry, and bring to room temperature before proceeding.

3. In a large skillet over medium heat, melt the butter with the oil. When the mixture is foamy, add the shallots and cook until golden brown, about 3 minutes. Raise the heat to high and add the beans, tossing to coat. Cook until the beans begin to color on the edges (don't move them around too much), about another 3 minutes. Add the lemon zest and juice, tossing to coat. Add salt and pepper to taste and serve immediately.

SERVES 2

FLASH HOME-FRIES

Bake the potatoes earlier in the day (or the day before) and refrigerate them. Cold potatoes are easier to cut and hold together better in the skillet. If the potatoes don't have a lot of moisture and start sticking, you might want to add another tablespoon each of butter and oil.

> **2 large Idaho potatoes (as uniform as possible, about 10 oz. each), scrubbed but not peeled**
> **2 tablespoons unsalted butter**
> **1 tablespoon olive oil**
> **¼ cup diced red onion**
> **Kosher salt and coarsely-ground black pepper to taste**
> **2 tablespoons finely chopped flat-leaf parsley**

1. Preheat the oven to 375°F.

2. Halve the potatoes lengthwise and place them cut-side up directly on the oven rack. Bake until the entire (top) surface of the potatoes has a golden-brown crust and the tip of a paring knife easily pierces the underside, 35 to 40 minutes. Let the potatoes cool until they are easy to handle, then cut into large dice (about 3 cups).

3. Melt the butter with the oil in a heavy skillet over medium-high heat. When the mixture is foamy, add the onions and cook until the edges begin to color, about 3 minutes. Add the potatoes, tossing to coat, and cook until heated through (turn only once or twice so they get a chance to crisp), 6 to 8 minutes. Liberally salt and pepper the potatoes, adding the parsley just before serving.

SERVES 2

GIVING GOOD HOST: FLOWER POWER

Just one word describes the best kind of floral decoration: nonchalant. A stiff, formal "centerpiece" that looks like something you might find in a hotel lobby can take the fun out of any table setting. Even if you have little floral sense (and even less occasion to come in contact with a florist who does), it doesn't take much to pull off a simple but sophisticated style: Think supper club.

Buy a few small vases (none taller than six inches). Since stems are the ugliest part of a flower, consider something other than clear glass, such as earthenware or ceramic. The narrower the opening, the more tightly the stems will be held together, allowing the blooms to spread. Another good choice is a timeless silver or silverplate mint julep cup.

Pick a prearranged bouquet. These days, upscale "bucket shops" and flower stalls in fancy food markets sell "instant arrangements" that are a cut above the standard bunched flowers. Pick the most natural looking (no tiny blue carnations).

Make the cut. Working in proportions of one-third flowers to two-thirds container, cut the stems and place the prearranged bouquet in your vase. Fluff the flowers to loosen them and make the arrangement look more relaxed. That's it: little, low and very stylish flowers

2/Moroccan Lamb Shanks with Orange and Olive Gremolata ➤ Middle Eastern Quesadillas

Although I'm not the kind of woman who seduces men with fabulous lingerie and flawless grooming, spending all my time buffing and waxing and straddling a lacy thong, my specialty is just as labor-intensive and almost as deceptive. I am the mistress of the make-ahead meal: food that never reveals the effort that went into its preparation; "social food," calling for nothing more taxing than conversation. "Can I get you something?" I might ask, casually pulling sliced steak, pickled shrimp or cold roast chicken out of my beautifully outfitted refrigerator.

However, as any lingerie lover will tell you, into each relationship some flannel must eventually fall. In my case, this translates into the night when, exhausted by the strain of all that clandestine cooking, I finally put it all out there on the table—letting the man see that a certain amount of domestic drudgery goes into his nocturnal treats. The consequence of such a revelation can be only one of two things: the beginning, or the beginning of the end.

I usually open up with something very homey and cozy, like these lamb shanks, a Middle Eastern take on osso buco, the classic Milanese dish. (Osso buco—or *oss bus* in the dialect of Milan—means "bone with a hole.") It is traditionally made with veal shanks and served with *gremolata* (a garnish of finely chopped lemon zest, garlic, and parsley). With its long, slow cooking time—in a spice-infused liquid that fills my apartment with savory smells—braising lamb shanks is the culinary equivalent of commitment.

Stacking Textures

Although osso buco is usually served with risotto, I find that combination too consistently rich and creamy. Instead, I opt for a dish that has a separate textural identify by making a Middle Eastern interpretation of a Mexican quesadilla, and serving wedges of the pan-toasted tortillas alongside the shanks to soak up the sauce. Dessert: peanut butter cookies topped with a chocolate kiss (page 162) alongside vanilla ice cream with butterscotch sauce (page 166).

Social Scenario

Braising is not a precise science. It does not rely on split-second timing. It is a relaxed, grandmotherly way of cooking. Although you can't hide the cooking smells, the amount of time you actually have to spend in the kitchen (reducing the sauce and making the quesadillas) while guests are present is nothing compared to the deep, rich flavor you are able to produce. With their comfy domestic qualities, lamb shanks aren't actually a seduction meal. But they will work for an evening when you want your guests to feel at ease, or those times when you want to move a relationship a little closer.

Cooking Strategy

Before you braise the lamb, you must first brown the shanks and deglaze the pan. The lamb shanks are lightly coated with flour (called dredging) and then cooked over high heat until a crust forms. This is a messy but necessary step that will contribute greatly to the depth and richness of the sauce. Searing the shanks leaves little browned bits of meat and flour stuck to the bottom of the pan: These are very important in flavoring and thickening the sauce. You remove these browned bits by adding liquid (usually stock or wine) to the pan and stirring to loosen, incorporating them into the sauce: This is called *deglazing.* Pan juices are sometimes thickened by adding flour and butter (see Roast Chicken, page 60), but here they are just simmered to reduce and thicken them.

It is difficult to reheat quesadillas, so you can't make them ahead. However, once finished, you can keep them warm in the oven (which will still be hot from cooking the lamb shanks) while you make the sauce for the lamb. Keep back-up ingredients prepped and you can quickly make seconds to order.

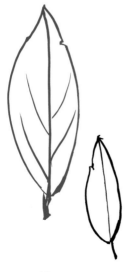

MOROCCAN LAMB SHANKS

Lamb shanks, cut from the foreleg, weigh about 1 pound each and may need to be ordered in advance from your butcher. Although I believe in serving the whole shank, some cooks find it awkward, so they have the butcher saw each shank crosswise into three pieces. Another sissified presentation is to cook the shank whole and then slide the tender cooked meat right off the bone and onto your plate. Either way, you lose the satisfying earthy sexiness of this dish, and you never learn the truth: Is this the kind of person who can step up to the plate and take matters into her own hands, big bones and all?

FOR THE ORANGE AND OLIVE GREMOLATA
    3 tablespoons chopped pitted Moroccan oil-cured black olives (about 16 olives)
    1 tablespoon finely chopped flat-leaf parsley
    1 tablespoon minced orange zest

FOR THE LAMB SHANKS
    ½ teaspoon whole cloves
    ½ teaspoon whole black peppercorns
    ½ teaspoon whole allspice
    1 bay leaf
    2 sprigs fresh thyme
    2 garlic cloves, peeled and smashed
    4 lamb shanks
    ½ cup flour for dredging
    2 tablespoons olive oil
    3 large shallots, peeled and roughly chopped
    2 cups superior beef stock
    ½ cup orange juice (no pulp)
    ½ cup dry red wine
    1 cup canned San Marzano tomatoes, crushed by hand, with their juices
    Kosher salt and ground black pepper to taste

1. For the Orange and Olive Gremolata, combine the olives, parsley, and orange zest in a small bowl. You can do this up to 4 hours ahead of time. Do not refrigerate.

2. Preheat the oven to 350°F. Place the spices, bay leaf, thyme, and garlic in a spice bag (a small muslin bag with drawstrings, available in any kitchen supply store) and set aside. Lightly coat the lamb shanks with flour, shaking off the excess.

3. In a large flameproof casserole over medium-high heat, warm the oil until hot but not smoking. Brown the lamb shanks on all sides.

4. Remove the lamb shanks and pour off all but 2 tablespoons of fat from the casserole. Add the shallots and cook, stirring occasionally, until the edges begin to color, about 3 minutes. Add the stock, juice, and wine, stirring to scrape up any browned bits from the bottom of the casserole. Add the tomatoes and stir to blend. Add the spice bag and bring the mixture to a boil. Return the shanks to the casserole, cover tightly, and place in the oven. Cook until the meat is very tender (it will shrink away from the bone, almost falling off), about 2 hours.

5. Carefully transfer the casserole to the stovetop; remove and discard the spice bag. Transfer the lamb shanks to a platter and cover loosely with foil. Over medium heat, bring the cooking liquid to a boil. Lower the heat and simmer until the liquid begins to thicken, 10 to 12 minutes. Season with salt and pepper.

6. Place each lamb shank in a large shallow bowl or deep-rimmed plate. Ladle sauce over the shanks and sprinkle with gremolata. Place several quesadilla wedges alongside each shank and serve, passing extra quesadillas on the side.

SERVES 4

THE EQUIPMENT: DUTCH OVEN
For braising, use a Dutch oven, a heavy casserole that's good for both stovetop browning and oven cooking. Made of enameled cast iron, stainless steel, or copper (which can go from stove to oven to table), the pan must have small handles on both sides and a tight-fitting lid to prevent evaporation and aid in the condensation of moisture.

To me, three words describe the perfect snack: *ready right now*. And quesadillas certainly qualify. Once you get the method down, vary the fillings (those suggested below, or your own creations) to make starters or late-night snacks in minutes.

1. Monterey Jack and salsa fresca (drained of extra liquid)

2. Shredded roast chicken, watercress, and soft goat cheese

3. Cooked ground beef or warmed leftover chili with Cheddar

4. Sliced andouille sausage or chorizo and pepper Jack

5. Sautéed portobello mushrooms with fontina

6. Thinly sliced sautéed shrimp and salsa verde with Mexican asadero cheese.

MIDDLE EASTERN QUESADILLAS

Arina is a semi-firm goat-milk gouda with a smooth texture and a mild but tangy taste. Use a cheese shaver or plane to make long, thin strips that will melt evenly and quickly. I've found that 8 shaver slices yield about 3 ounces.

2 (8-inch) flour tortillas
3 oz. goat gouda, such as Arina
¼ cup cleaned and stemmed arugula

1. Lightly coat a large nonstick skillet or griddle with cooking spray (wiping out the excess with a paper towel) and heat over medium heat. Place one tortilla in the skillet and layer with half the cheese. Evenly distribute the arugula on top, then add the remaining cheese. Top with the second tortilla, as though you were making a sandwich.

2. Place a heatproof plate on the top tortilla (to press the quesadilla together). Cook until the cheese melts and the quesadilla begins to stick together, about 2 minutes.

3. Remove the plate (potholders, please) and, using a spatula, flip the quesadilla to toast the second side. Replace the "weight" plate and cook for another minute or so; the second side will toast faster than the first.

4. Remove the plate and slide the quesadilla onto a cutting board. Cut into wedges and serve alongside the lamb shanks.

MAKES ONE 8-INCH QUESADILLA

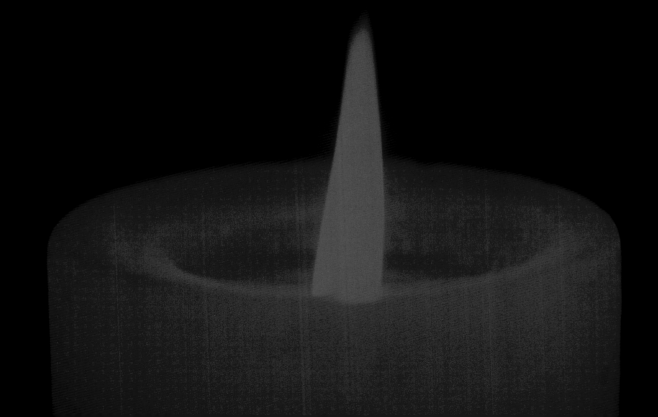

GIVING GOOD HOST: LIGHTING

After many catering years spent in rarified homes, I can tell you a few things about creating (and killing) a mood. But my favorite ambience advice came to me via lifestyle guru Lee Bailey: When Radio City Music Hall opened, in 1932, people were so audibly excited by the Art Deco design in the brightly lit lobby that their voices carried into the adjacent theater, disturbing audiences. An enlightened designer (who realized that the brighter the bulbs, the bigger the voices) told the management to dim the lobby lights to the lowest possible level—where they remain today—and conversations became hushed. Apply this theory to the lighting scheme in your own home. If you want intimacy (of conversation or anything else), keep the lamps low and the candles lit. I even keep a small, low-wattage lamp on in my kitchen so there is never a need to turn on the unflattering overheads. Try out your lighting scheme in advance (at the same hour that you are expecting guests) so you can see exactly what your place will look like on the night you are entertaining (will people still be able to see?). Have everything set by the time guests arrive. Giving people a glimpse into the machinery behind the mood by fiddling with the lights while they wait is more than distracting, it's deadly.

3/Seafood Risotto
➤ Fennel and Celery Salad

About twelve years ago, long before every Tom, Dick, and Dimitri could afford to go wireless, international restaurateur Harry Cipriani anticipated the day when piercing cell phone trills and shrills would reduce his chic café in New York's Sherry-Netherland Hotel into a party in a monkey cage. When Cipriani chose to discourage his moneyed monkeys with the explanation that "the ringing of cell phones interferes with the making of risotto," printed right on the menu, all I could think was *brilliant genius*. Not just because Cipriani cared enough about ambiance to make his very-paying customers turn off their phones; not even because he did it in such a charming and witty way. But because he did it in such an *Italian* way, by alluding to the mystical power of food, animating the inanimate—as though risotto has the temperament of a beautiful woman who must be properly wooed before she's won.

Whether it started at Harry Cipriani's or just flourished there, risotto's reputation as a difficult dish (all that stirring!) has been thoroughly established in America's mind, spawning long and stunningly boring cooking-magazine articles that unnecessarily complicate what is basically a straightforward recipe. When you get right down to it, two essential qualities will make you a risotto maestro: addiction to perfection (especially when it comes to ingredients) and patience.

Social Scenario

I was once infatuated with a guy who spent every day and every night in relentlessly chic restaurants. This guy not only wouldn't stay at home, he couldn't, terrified that doing so would make him a boring person *(big ego/low self-esteem)*. He was the classic free-range chicken: a roving man who couldn't commit *(attention-deficit dater)*. Plus he had that fancy little wine salesman nose and couldn't abide cooking smells —they reeked of domesticity *(mother issues)*. In order to keep him in (and interested) at night, I had to devise the perfect kitchen seduction.

This seafood risotto worked for me; here's how to make it work for you.

Maintain a casual air. When your guest asks, "What time do you want me?" you can reply, "Whenever you like." And when she arrives, there's no frantic evidence of dinner hanging in the air, no trace of desperation or eagerness to impress. All the basic prep work is done so far in advance that any evidence of your labor is long gone.

Take your sweet time. Everything is ready and waiting, so chat her up; hang out for a while and compliment her on her shoes. Let her expectation build a little before you finally take her into the kitchen and show her what you've got.

Turn it on. If you let your guest sit in your pristine kitchen, marveling at your effortless competence, you'll develop a reputation as a man who can flirt and make a fabulous meal all at once. And let me assure you, when a man is good with his hands, especially at something as basic as satisfying a woman's hunger, well, that's heartthrob territory.

Stacking Textures

You can't just plunk a green salad down on the table after a dish as velvety as seafood risotto. Where's the fun (or the flavor) in that? Instead, use a quick toss of fennel and celery as a refreshing palate adjuster. Dessert: Move away from the table, and pass some chocolate truffles at just the right moment (see How to Buy Truffles, Page 169).

Cooking Strategy

This is a three-part dish. Early in the day, prep the seafood. You can even measure out the rice, stock and spices, storing them in separate bowls so they're ready when needed. Just before you start the risotto, remove the precooked salmon and lobster meat from the refrigerator (to take the chill off—they are only briefly warmed before serving). Pour a couple of glasses of wine and begin the risotto. Just before the rice is cooked, sauté the scallops and lobster. For the grand finale, arrange the seafood over the rice.

HOW TO BUY SCALLOPS

Although larger than gumdrop-size bay scallops, sea scallops are still extremely fragile and highly perishable. Look for plump, firm scallops with a creamy beige color. In the market, they should be displayed on crushed ice and not in water (the scallops absorb the water, upping their weight and making them more expensive). When scallops are too wet, they leak excess water and steam rather than sear, ending up like tough, expensive erasers.

SEAFOOD RISOTTO

Making risotto is a slow process and you can't rush it. If you find the rice is absorbing the liquid too quickly (in less than 10 to 12 minutes for the first addition and about 8 minutes thereafter), the heat is too high. This particular risotto is loaded with pricey seafood and will serve two ambitious eaters as a generous main course. Over the years, it has become one of my signature dishes. Although I could probably make it in my sleep, I never let on that it's easy. (And you will probably find that it gets easier for you, too, with practice.) Instead, I just stir and smile, relying on risotto's temperamental reputation to do the rest, impressing my guest and making Harry proud.

FOR THE SEAFOOD:
    1½ lb. steamed lobster (many fish counters will steam the lobster for you,
        or you can do it yourself)
    6 ounces salmon fillet, skinned
    ½ lb. sea scallops (at least 6)
    ½ lb. large shrimp (at least 12)
    ½ lemon, thinly sliced
    1 teaspoon black peppercorns
    2 stems fresh chives

FOR THE RISOTTO:
    3 cups superior chicken stock mixed with ½ cup reserved fish stock
        and 1 cup water
    1 tablespoon plus 2 teaspoons unsalted butter
    2 shallots, finely chopped
    1 cup arborio rice
    ⅓ cup brut Champagne

FOR THE SEAFOOD SAUTE:
    About 2 tablespoons unsalted butter
    About 2 tablespoons olive oil
    Ground black pepper and coarse or kosher salt

THE END:
    ½ cup hand-grated Parmigiano-Reggiano
    1 teaspoon minced lemon zest
    1 tablespoon snipped fresh chives

1. To prep the seafood, use kitchen scissors to cut off the tips of the lobster claws, then hold the lobster upside down to drain trapped cooking water. Place the salmon in a small glass baking dish (do not use metal). Rinse the scallops; pat dry with paper towels. Peel and devein the shrimp, reserving the shells. Pick and shred the lobster meat into large chunks (about 1½ cups), reserving the shells.

2. Place the lobster and shrimp shells in a medium stockpot with 8 cups of water, the lemon slices, peppercorns, and chives, and bring to a boil. Simmer for at least 20 minutes, or until the liquid is infused with flavor. Ladle the simmering liquid over the salmon until the fish is submerged. Cover tightly and let the salmon sit until cooked but still translucent in the center, about 12 minutes. Drain the poaching liquid through a fine-mesh sieve and reserve ½ cup for the risotto. Refrigerate all the seafood.

3. Set the cooked seafood out to come to room temperature. Meanwhile, start cooking the risotto. In a heavy medium saucepan, bring the stock and water to a boil. Lower the heat and keep the mixture warm through the entire cooking process. In a medium stockpot over medium heat, melt the butter until foamy. Add the shallots and sauté until soft and lightly colored, about 3 minutes. Add the rice and stir with a wooden spoon until every grain is coated with melted butter. Add the Champagne and stir until absorbed.

THE EQUIPMENT: STOCKPOT, SAUCEPAN, WOODEN SPOON
The cooking equipment needed for risotto is not extensive: a sturdy medium-size stockpot (about 8 quarts), a saucepan, and a big-bowled wooden spoon with a long handle (16 to 18 inches) that keeps your hand out of the steaming rice. This is especially important because you are going to be stirring for a long time, allowing the rice to release its starch and thicken the stock until you have a smooth consistency and rice that is tender but still slightly firm to the bite (al dente).

4. Add 1 cup of hot stock and cook, stirring constantly, until the liquid is absorbed, 10 to 12 minutes; use broad strokes, lifting the rice up and off the bottom of the pot as you stir. Continue to cook the rice, adding ½ cup of hot stock at a time and stirring until the liquid is absorbed. The cooking process will take 30 to 40 minutes; the rice should be tender but still slightly firm to the bite.

5. When the risotto has absorbed most of the stock, sauté the shrimp and scallops. In a small skillet over low heat, melt 1 tablespoon of butter with 1 tablespoon of oil until foamy. Raise the heat to medium-high. The key to cooking shrimp and scallops is a hot pan: Adjust the heat so the pan is hot enough to immediately sear the surface of the scallops. When the butter mixture is lightly browned, add the scallops, sprinkle with pepper and cook until golden, about 2 minutes per side. With a slotted spoon, transfer the scallops to a plate and set aside.

6. Add more butter and oil to the skillet if necessary, and cook the shrimp as above. Do not overcook; the seafood should still look translucent in the center. Transfer the shrimp to a plate. Wipe out the skillet, reduce the heat, and melt 1 tablespoon of butter. Gently warm the lobster meat—it will only take seconds and should be done at the last possible moment.

7. To finish the dish, remove the risotto from the heat, sprinkle the cheese over the surface, and stir to incorporate. Add salt to taste, if necessary. Gently fold in the salmon. Spoon risotto into the center of each warmed plate. Arrange the lobster meat on top and the shrimp and scallops around the edges. Sprinkle with the lemon zest and chives.

SERVES 2 AS A MAIN COURSE, 4 AS A FIRST COURSE

THE BEST RICE, STOCK, AND CHEESE FOR RISOTTO

Although there are countless variations on the theme, risotto has only three basic ingredients, so quality is of the utmost importance: imported Italian arborio rice, the best stock you can buy, and Parmigiano-Reggiano.

1. ARBORIO RICE has a large, plump, pearly-white grain containing a high proportion of amylopectin, a starch that dissolves with cooking. Arborio rice is available in most large supermarkets, Italian groceries, and specialty food stores.

2. SUPERIOR STOCK is a prime flavoring agent. Whether your recipe calls for beef, chicken, vegetable, or seafood stock, its quality is vital to a good risotto. Although you can stop short of making your own stock, don't just settle for something from a can. Your butcher or fishmonger may make and sell their own stock, or you might be able to buy frozen stock concentrate in specialty food stores. Look for all-natural free-range chicken stock in a shelf-stable box at fancy supermarkets.

3. PARMIGIA NO-REGGIANO is a singular artisan-made, amber-hued cheese with a nutty, slightly salty flavor and grainy texture. Made in only two regions of Italy (Parma and Reggio Emilia); the words "Parmigiano-Reggiano" stenciled on the rind are the mark of authenticity.

GIVING GOOD HOST: SEATING FOR TWO

It isn't the size; it isn't the shape—it's how you use it. When you invite someone to dinner with seduction on your mind, always configure the table so that you and your guest sit side by side (so French), or catercorner at one end (so cozy), instead of directly across from each other in face-the-executioner style.

FENNEL AND CELERY SALAD

Called finocchio in Italy, fennel is a stalk vegetable, like celery or rhubarb, with a refreshing, slightly sweet taste reminiscent of anise or licorice. It can be eaten raw or cooked. Whether you slice the fennel horizontally or vertically doesn't matter; what's important is that you slice it finely. Oddly enough, the thinner you cut raw fennel, the better it tastes. When the slices are too thick, the flavor can be overpowering. Kitchen professionals often use a mandoline (a sharp, scary slicer with a taste for fingertips), but the time-consuming job can also be done with a sharp knife and a steady hand; it just takes practice. Toast the nuts and slice the fennel and celery in advance, but don't dress the salad until you are ready to serve.

> 2 tablespoons chopped walnuts
> 1 large fennel bulb (to yield 2 cups finely sliced fennel)
> 4 stalks celery (to yield 2 cups finely sliced celery)
> 1 tablespoon olive oil
> 1 teaspoon balsamic vinegar
> Coarse or kosher salt and ground black pepper to taste
> 2 tablespoons crumbled blue cheese (Roquefort or Danish Blue)

1. Preheat the oven to 350°F. Place two salad plates in the refrigerator to chill.

2. Spread the walnuts in a small baking pan and toast in the oven until golden, 4 to 6 minutes (when you start to smell them, they are done). Immediately tip the toasted nuts into a plate so they do not continue to cook from retained heat.

3. Trim the feathery fronds and hollow stalks from the fennel, leaving just the bulb. Discard the tough outer leaves and cut the bulb in half. Rest each half on its flat side and finely slice the fennel. Trim, rinse and dry the celery stalks. Finely slice on the diagonal.

4. Place the celery and fennel in a glass or ceramic bowl. At serving time, drizzle the vegetables with oil and toss. When the celery and fennel are thoroughly coated, add the vinegar and repeat. (Adding the oil first keeps the pale green fennel from being stained by the dark balsamic vinegar.) Add salt and pepper to taste. Transfer the salad to the chilled serving plates and sprinkle with the walnuts and blue cheese.

SERVES 2

59

4/Roast Chicken
➤ Skillet Asparagus
➤ Mashed Reds

For the last twenty years, telling New Yorkers what to eat has been my business. As a high-end caterer I have prepared every sort of meal, from intimate dinners in elaborate private homes to splashy sit-downs at the Guggenheim Museum. And over those many years, it has also been my pleasure to tell New Yorkers *where* to eat, happily answering questions about "who makes the best what" and providing restaurant advice by matching the specific occasion to the perfect location. But lately, when New Yorkers ask me where I like to go for dinner, my response is that on the whole, I would rather eat in Philadelphia.

Sure, Manhattan has some unbelievable expense-account and tourist-destination restaurants. But as far as medium-expensive mainstream restaurants where a city's fulltime residents go to spend their own money, I find those in Philadelphia more interesting. It's not just the food. There's a difference in the way the restaurants look and feel, a difference that I believe can be traced to the way the two cities define urban renewal.

While New York generally focuses on the "new," Philadelphia concentrates on the "re"—recycling, restoring, and rethinking how best to use its city spaces. Manhattan restaurateurs gut a building to build a big blank box and then, like *nouveaux riches* who hang portraits of somebody else's ancestors, use salvaged architectural details as a decorative afterthought. But in a city as old as Philadelphia, where everything was once something else, buildings are allowed to have longer lives. When existing architecture is allowed to drive new design, the result is quirkier spaces with a luster of authenticity that all the money in Manhattan can't buy.

I have a favorite: the Blue Angel, Philadelphia restaurateur Steven Starr's flawless rendition of a classic French brasserie, complete with zinc bar, tarnished mercury mirrors, and a luminous milk-glass ceiling (a turn-of-the-century feature original to the building). This roast chicken recipe is styled on the Blue Angel's *poulet roti,* a partially boned, roasted chicken breast served in a shallow bowl with natural pan juices. Although brasserie classics (like steak *frites* and roast chicken) have become ubiquitous, they remain an excellent way to judge the overall quality—the integrity—of a kitchen. There's no hiding behind fancy sauces with a straightforward dish like roast chicken; it takes focus to produce a bird with crispy skin and tender, juicy meat, and being able to make one in your own kitchen is the ultimate test of a good home cook.

Social Scenario

There's a reason why I am willing to pay a premium price for roast chicken in restaurants—it can be a mess to make at home. The timing, the carving, the pan juices—just trying to get everything to the table while it is still warm is like a mini-Thanksgiving. Yes, your guests will love you for it (because chicken roasted at home really does taste different/better.) But it will be a kitchen free-for-all during the last few minutes before you serve, making this a meal to save for guests who are more like family than friends.

Stacking Textures

Would the roast chicken be better paired with a crisp potato gratin? Maybe. But try telling people that you were going to make mashed potatoes but thought the texture was a little too rich for the rest of the meal. This is a classic case of just going with what people like (maybe the lumps in the potatoes are all the texture they need). Dessert: Continue the fantasy that this is a family meal (with less fighting and better wine). Serve an assorted cookie plate with the added attraction of chocolate espresso bourbon brownies (page 155).

Cooking Strategy

Don't let the mashed potatoes sit in the pot over burner heat (no matter how low). To keep them warm while you put the finishing touches on the rest of the meal, cover the pot and place it in a low oven (probably still warm from roasting the chicken). The heat may make the potatoes rise slightly (sort of like a soufflé), but at least they won't burn on the bottom.

ROAST CHICKEN

Use a shallow roasting pan in which the chickens fit snugly so that the pan juices collect instead of spreading out and evaporating. Using smaller chickens allows you to give each person half of the bird, which means the guest gets a little of everything, dark and white meat.

THE CHICKENS

    4 (6-inch) rosemary stalks
    4 tablespoons olive oil
    4 tablespoons unsalted butter
    1 teaspoon soy sauce
    4 garlic cloves, peeled and smashed
    2 (2½-lb.) chickens (called fryers or broilers, available from the butcher)
    1 lemon, cut into 8 wedges
    16 whole black peppercorns
    1 teaspoon coarse or kosher salt

THE SAUCE

    3⅓ cups superior chicken stock
    ⅔ cup dry vermouth
    2 tablespoons unsalted butter, at room temperature
    2 tablespoons all-purpose flour

1. Preheat the oven to 375°F. Strip the needles from two of the rosemary stalks. Discard the stems.

2. Combine the oil, butter, soy sauce, garlic, and rosemary needles in a small saucepan over medium heat. Heat until the mixture foams and the butter begins to brown, about 3 minutes; the rosemary needles will get crisp. Scoop out the rosemary and reserve for garnish. Using tongs, remove the garlic cloves and reserve; set aside the pan.

3. Rinse the chickens (inside and out) under cool running water and pat dry with paper towels. Fill the cavity of each chicken with half the lemon wedges, the remaining rosemary stalks, reserved garlic, the peppercorns, and salt, then

THE EQUIPMENT: WIRE WHISK
The best tool for deglazing a pan is a lightweight, heat-resistant flat (soft) wire whisk that enables you to make sauce right in the pan without splattering.

place the birds on a v-shaped roasting rack in a shallow roasting pan. Using a basting brush, coat the birds (on all sides and in crevices) with the butter-oil mixture from the saucepan. Roast until the skin is crisp and the meat is thoroughly cooked but still juicy, 55 to 60 minutes. (An instant-read meat thermometer inserted in the thickest part of the thigh should read 165–170°F.) About halfway through, rotate the pan so the chickens brown on all sides.

4. To make the sauce, in a small saucepan over medium heat, bring the stock and vermouth to a boil. Reduce the heat and simmer until the liquid is reduced by about half, 10 to 12 minutes. Meanwhile, mash the butter and flour to form a paste.

5. When the chickens are done, transfer them to a cutting board and let rest at least 10 minutes before carving. Meanwhile, make the sauce. Pour off the excess fat from the roasting pan and deglaze the pan (see page 45) with the hot stock mixture, using a flat sauce whisk to scrape up any browned bits. Return the mixture to the saucepan and bring to a simmer over medium heat. Bit by bit, whisk in the butter-flour paste. Simmer until the sauce is thickened, 8 minutes. Once you have added the butter, do not let the sauce boil.

6. To carve the chickens, use a sharp, heavy knife to separate the legs and thighs from the wing portion. Then, slide a knife with a thinner, more supple blade down each side of the breastbone, scooping out the breast section and leaving the skin intact if possible. Each chicken will serve two people. Top with the pan sauce, sprinkle with fried rosemary, and serve.

SERVES 4

THE EQUIPMENT: ROASTING RACK
A v-shaped roasting rack holds the bird together as it cooks, eliminating the need for trussing. Look for a sturdy rack with a nonstick surface (so the skin doesn't tear) and a design that makes it easy to grip (so you can lift the bird from the roasting pan to the carving board without any trouble). Get an adjustable rack to insure that the birds will be held snugly, but not too tightly.

SKILLET ASPARAGUS

In my catering kitchen, we called this "railroading" asparagus because it speeds up the cooking process. When you do it right, the water clinging to the stalks steams the asparagus while the butter/oil combination browns them, bringing out the best flavor.

> 1 tablespoon unsalted butter
> 1 tablespoon olive oil
> 2 shallots, peeled and minced
> 1½ lb. medium-thin asparagus (about 36 stalks)
> Coarse or kosher salt and ground black pepper

1. In a large, heavy skillet with a tight-fitting lid, melt the butter with the oil over medium heat until foamy. Add the shallots and cook, stirring frequently, until golden brown, about 3 minutes.

2. Trim the asparagus and rinse under cool running water. Do not drain. Add the asparagus (with water still clinging to the stalks) to the skillet. Using long tongs, quickly rotate the asparagus to coat. Cover tightly and cook, turning once or twice, until the asparagus is lightly colored but still crisp-tender, about 4 minutes.

3. Season with salt and pepper and serve immediately, topping each portion with some of the browned shallots.

SERVES 4

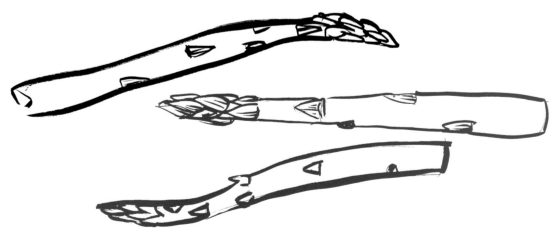

MASHED REDS

Red potatoes, especially the smaller ones, produce a less gluey and slightly sweeter, "fresher" tasting mashed potato.

> 2 lb. red potatoes (as unblemished as possible), scrubbed but not peeled and cut into uniform chunks (about 2 inches)
> 4 to 5 tablespoons butter at room temperature, cut into small pieces (it's easiest to cut the butter while cold and then let it come to room temperature)
> ¾ to 1 cup heavy cream, at room temperature
> 2 tablespoons snipped chives
> 2 tablespoons finely chopped flat-leaf parsley
> Coarse or kosher salt and ground black pepper

1. Place a colander in the sink. Put the potatoes in a small stockpot and cover with at least 6 inches of cold water. Bring to a boil over medium heat and boil until the potatoes are tender enough for a sharp knife blade to pierce the center, 20 to 25 minutes. (Do not overcook the potatoes or they will be mushy.)

2. Working quickly, remove the pot from the heat and drain the potatoes in the colander, shaking it gently. Immediately return the potatoes to the hot pot (but do not return the pot to the heat).

3. Using a whisk or hand-held potato masher (do not use an electric mixer), break the potatoes into smaller pieces. Mash the butter, piece by piece, into the potatoes, then make a well in the center, adding the cream a little at a time and mashing it into the potatoes. The potatoes should be slightly lumpy. You may have to bang the whisk on the side of the pot a few times to release any bits of potato trapped in the center.

4. Fold the chives and parsley into the potatoes and season with salt and pepper to taste.

SERVES 4

5/Peppered Tuna
➤ Spinach with Garlic
➤ Popcorn New Potatoes

I once fell in love with a guy so tragically wrong for me that our entire relationship verged on opera. What possessed me can be summed up in two words: wine salesman. For those who have never seen the ceremony of wine performed by an initiate, I will swear to the magic in its rituals—the offhanded swirling and tilt of the glass towards the candlelight, that first tentative sip. But it was the language that seduced me: wine lists that read like romance novels, the thrill of seeing a grown man stick his nose in a glass and come up with a word like *jammy,* the shameless eroticism in the wine taste and wine talk. When this guy leaned across the table, looked at me and said, "I like mine full-bodied, with long legs and an endless, silky finish," I had never heard such a sentence—at least not from a man still wearing his pants. Suddenly the thought of asking a waiter, "What kind of wine do you have by the glass?" took on the childish cadence of a knock-knock joke.

As it goes in many shaky relationships, the wine salesman and I found stability in a triangle, making it a practice to attend important wine dinners accompanied by his closest friend, the mastermind behind many of the city's most exciting wine lists and a man who brought out the best in both of us. With the friend as my table companion during those long wine-soaked evenings, the salesman was free to wheedle his clients into spending huge sums of money while I had someone interesting enough to help keep me conscious. And sane.

Because something happens when wine is tasted *en masse.* As the number of people and bottles grows, the intimacy is replaced by a competitive quest for the most extravagant description, often accompanied by alarming mouth noises. During one endless dinner in a flashy restaurant known for its elaborate preparations of fish, the waiter approached and began his merciless recitation of the chef's specials. The friend, sitting by my side and mindful of the fact that my entire food philosophy can be summed up with the phrase "sizzle platter," cut the waiter short by saying, "Bring her a two-inch cut of tuna. And cook it like a steak."

For those accustomed to more exotic preparations (that take longer to explain), this pepper-crusted, firm piece of rare tuna may not seem exciting. But people like me, whose hearty appetites are rarely satisfied by fish, will be thrilled by its convenient duality: the political correctness of fish with the staying power of meat.

Stacking Textures
Even though the flavors are refined, there is a rough, hearty quality to this meal. It is a perfect plate: The pepper-crusted fish, no longer such a delicate thing, is set off by crisp potatoes and the richness of the sautéed spinach. Dessert: Poached oranges (page 153) served with some exotic ice cream (like pumpkin), and ginger-spice cookies (page 163).

Social Scenario
This menu can be seen as representing the Triple Crown of cooking: Efficient. Effective. Impressive.

If you don't think there's anything attractive about a man who can whip it together thirty minutes after he walks through the front door, think again.

PEPPERED TUNA

A nonstick skillet (see page 41) is essential; the surface "releases" the fish without tearing the crust. Don't skimp on the oil. It must be deep enough to submerge the pepper crust (not the entire tuna steak). Unless the peppercorns are fried in the hot oil, they will taste unpleasantly "raw" and sharp. The exact amount of oil you'll need depends on the size of your skillet.

FOR EACH SERVING:
   2 tablespoons whole black peppercorns, cracked
   2 teaspoons coarse or kosher salt
   ½ lb. tuna steak (cut from the narrow end of the loin that tapers near the tail), about 2 inches thick
   Vegetable oil

1. Combine the pepper and salt on a plate and press the tuna into the mixture to coat both sides.

2. Cover the bottom of a large nonstick skillet with a pool of oil and heat over medium-high heat until hot but not smoking. Using tongs, place the tuna in the pan and sear until a crust forms, turning only once. Approximately 3 minutes total cooking time will give you rare tuna; 4 minutes for medium-rare. (Tuna cooked beyond medium-rare can be very dry.)

3. To serve: Leave the tuna steak whole, or slice it thickly on the diagonal, fanning the pieces out slightly on the plate to display the contrast between the smooth red interior and the dark peppery crust.

SERVES 4

USE EVERYTHING
Toast slices of country bread on a rack in a pre-heated 375°F oven. Transfer to serving plates and spread with softened garlic cloves. Top with sautéed spinach and curls of salty Parmigiano-Reggiano (made by dragging a swivel-head vegetable peeler across the face of a wedge of cheese).

SPINACH WITH GARLIC

This cooking technique is akin to "railroading" asparagus. The trick here is to have just enough water clinging to the leaves, and the butter and oil hot enough, so that the spinach wilts without becoming too "slippery." Only practice can teach you how to get it just right.

2 tablespoons unsalted butter
1 tablespoon olive oil
4 garlic cloves, peeled and smashed
2 bunches fresh spinach (about 2 lb. total weight), trimmed and well rinsed but not dried
Coarse or kosher salt and ground black pepper

1. Combine the butter and oil in a large skillet with a tight-fitting lid over medium-high heat, and heat until foamy.

2. Add the garlic and sauté until lightly browned, about 3 minutes. Immediately add the damp spinach. Using long tongs, quickly toss the spinach to coat it. Cover tightly and cook until the spinach is wilted, about 3 minutes.

3. Add salt and pepper to taste and serve, discarding the garlic if desired.

SERVES 4

POPCORN NEW POTATOES

Tiny red potatoes, called "creamers," are often sold in small mesh bags, so you can see that the potatoes are unblemished and of uniform size. For this recipe you'll need a heavy pot large enough to hold the potatoes in a single layer; it must also have a tight-fitting lid to hold in the steam.

24 of the smallest (uniform) red potatoes (about 1¾ lb.)
2 tablespoons unsalted butter
Coarse or kosher salt and ground black pepper

1. Using a vegetable peeler or paring knife, pare a "belt" around the circumference of each potato. Wash the potatoes but do not drain excess water.

2. In a large, heavy pot with a tight-fitting lid, melt the butter over medium-high heat until foamy and almost browned. Place the wet potatoes in the pot and cover tightly.

3. When you hear the potatoes begin to sizzle, about 3 minutes (depending on the size of the potatoes and the weight of the pot), check to see if they are starting to brown. If they are, shake the pot (holding the lid tightly as though making popcorn) every few minutes to turn them. Start checking for doneness in 15 to 18 minutes. The potatoes are done when the tip of sharp knife pierces them easily. Season with salt and pepper to taste.

SERVES 4

HOW TO SET THE TABLE

Brasserie meals seem more charming and relaxed than those in other kinds of restaurants. It's not the food (which can be quite complex); it's something in the atmosphere and in the way the food is served. Authentic brasserie dining usually means a very simple table set-up, no matter how expensive the place might be. So forget the fancy party plates and matchy-matchy table setting ideas you see in magazines. Restaurant-supply companies (and lifestyle home stores) sell brasserie-style tableware: big white plates with thick rims and slightly indented centers, reasonably priced reproductions of plain, heavy hotel silver (that doesn't even have to match), and 18- or 22-inch square unadorned white cotton napkins. These little touches can instantly bring any table setting comfortably down to earth, no matter how extravagant the meal or important the guests.

6/Lamb Kebabs *or* Oven-Roasted Lamb Chops *or* Rack of Lamb
➤ Almond-Parsley Pilaf
➤ Romaine and Dill Salad

Growing up in the late fifties in Ankara, Turkey, I had a fabulous, romantic childhood—free to wander through the narrow passageways of the covered bazaars (all that coffee!) listening to the rhythm of marketplace bartering that turned the exchange of money into an intimate act, and enjoying more than my share of Middle Eastern street food, including the omnipresent meat on a stick: *sis kebab* (grilled cubes of meat) and *doner kebab* (rolls of spiced ground lamb). In that part of the world, where the Mediterranean meets Asia, meat is a valuable commodity, and every oddly-shaped bit is threaded onto a skewer, often served on a bed of rice so the cooking juices drip down and flavor the grain.

In this country, however, kebabs are more about style and convenience than tradition or economy. Skewering cubes of meat not only saves cooking and carving time; serving kebabs means guests can stand (if they have to) and eat with knife-free ease.

Stacking Textures

As with most Turkish food, the beautiful balance of color and flavor and texture makes even this simple meal seem like a feast. Despite America's preoccupation with exotic (and often sticky-sweet) marinades, lamb needs only a simple mixture, not to flavor the meat but to enhance the flavor that is already there. The lemon juice and rosemary in this marinade do not alter as much as lighten the lamb, cutting through the rich creaminess of the meat (which the misguided often refer to as "greasy").

While the romaine salad may not be as famous as a "Greek" salad, it is another clean-tasting Mediterranean combination with a bit of a bite, designed to balance the richness of the lamb and the rice. It even looks

72

refreshing: chartreuse-tipped romaine leaves set off by dark-green dill and silvery green onions. (To fill out the menu, serve feta cheese and good black olives on the side.)

Since romaine stays crisp longer than most salad greens, and the rice pilaf absorbs and holds the meat juices, this meal can be all served on one plate (like the Tex-Mex combo platters that have a main course, rice, beans, and greens) making it work *pour deux* or as buffet-style party food. Dessert: With food this bright and fresh, absolutely anything works.

Social Scenario

Casual, casual, casual: When you are serving kebabs, take advantage of Turkey's nomadic tradition to move your guest(s) wherever you want. Start out at the table, end up on the couch—from the Golden Globes to the Oscars, there is no better television-watching, long-drawn-out-awards-evening meal.

Cooking Strategy

If you are serving the kebabs at a seated party, transfer each skewer directly to a plate. However, when serving from a buffet, the lamb will be easier for guests to manage if you take the meat off the skewers (by sliding each skewer between the tines of fork). There you have it: my own Middle Eastern strategy.

LAMB KEBABS

Once the meat is out of the marinade, thread it snugly onto skewers without overcrowding: Fitting the lamb cubes together too tightly will prevent them from cooking evenly. Use the marinated onions to separate some of the chunks of lamb. Although the onions will cook quickly and add their own charred sweetness, resist the temptation to add other ingredients, such as mushrooms or eggplant, to the skewers. Juggling different cooking times can mean well-done lamb and raw vegetables (or vice versa).

3 lb. well-trimmed boneless shoulder or leg of lamb, cut into 1½-inch cubes
3 small red onions, peeled and quartered
½ cup fresh lemon juice
4 tablespoons olive oil
4 tablespoons finely chopped fresh rosemary needles (three 6-inch stalks)
2 teaspoons coarse or kosher salt
2 teaspoons ground black pepper

1. In a large glass or ceramic bowl, toss the lamb and onions with the remaining ingredients. Let stand at room temperature for 2 hours.

2. Preheat the broiler (or prepare a medium-hot charcoal or gas grill). Have ready 8 flat metal skewers.

3. Remove the lamb and onions from the marinade and slide them onto the skewers. Broil them (on the rack closest to the heat) or grill them (over a medium-hot fire), turning only once. If you are grilling the kebabs, brush them occasionally with marinade. In about 10 minutes you will have medium-rare lamb, and that's the way it should be served: charred on the outside, juicy and pink inside.

SERVES 4

THE EQUIPMENT: SKEWERS
Metal skewers will conduct heat through the center of the lamb much better than bamboo. Use flat skewers (so the kebabs don't spin around) 10 to 12 inches long.

ALMOND-PARSLEY PILAF

Rinsing the rice under hot water after cooking can seem like an odd step. But it makes for fluffier rice, creating a better—more absorbent—base for the kebabs.

½ cup sliced almonds
1 cup long-grain white rice, rinsed under cool running water
3 cups superior chicken stock
4 tablespoons unsalted butter
1 tablespoon olive oil
1 pint grape (or teardrop) tomatoes, stemmed, rinsed, and halved
2 shallots, finely chopped
¼ cup finely chopped flat-leaf parsley
1 teaspoon coarse or kosher salt
1 teaspoon ground black pepper

1. Preheat the oven to 350°F. Spread the almonds in a small baking pan and toast in the oven until golden, 4 to 6 minutes. When you start to smell the almonds, they are done; tip them from the pan into a plate so they don't overcook.

2. Combine the rice and stock in a medium saucepan and bring to a rolling boil over medium-high heat. Reduce the heat slightly, cover, and continue to simmer until the rice is tender, about 10 minutes. (The rice may be done before all the liquid is absorbed.) Transfer the rice to a colander, rinse with hot water, and drain.

3. While the rice is cooking, in a small skillet over medium heat melt 1 tablespoon of the butter with the oil until foamy. Add the tomatoes and quickly toss to coat, cooking only until the tomatoes are warmed through and their skins begin to pucker, about 3 minutes. Transfer the tomatoes to a plate and set aside.

4. Return the skillet to medium heat and add the remaining 3 tablespoons of butter. When the butter foams, add the shallots and cook until golden brown, about 3 minutes. Add the rice and stir to coat with butter. Sprinkle with the toasted almonds, parsley, salt and pepper. Add the tomatoes and stir gently to combine.

SERVES 4

ROMAINE AND DILL SALAD

The romaine must be bone dry; even a little surface water will rob this salad of its fresh crispness. Wash the lettuce ahead of time, shake or spin it dry, and wrap it in a kitchen towel. Refrigerate the lettuce in the crisper drawer until needed.

8 cups chopped romaine leaves (about 2 small heads, washed and dried)
⅓ cup chopped fresh dill
¼ cup finely sliced green onions
3 tablespoons olive oil
3 tablespoons fresh lemon juice, strained
Coarse or kosher salt and ground black pepper

Place the romaine, dill, and green onions in a large mixing bowl. Toss with the oil and lemon juice. Add salt and pepper to taste. Transfer to serving plates.

SERVES 4

The Three Levels of Lamb

Maybe your childhood wasn't spent wandering through the streets of Turkey eating meat off a stick, but it shouldn't take you long to figure out that lamb is a good alternative to beef. The pricier cuts (see How To Buy Lamb, page 46) are also easy to prepare. Even the most undomesticated piece of female frolic ever to hit the screen, Joan Crawford's character Crystal Allen (in director George Cukor's 1939 adaptation of Clare Booth Luce's play, *The Women*) knew the deal: "If you throw a lamb chop in the oven, what's to keep it from getting done?"

Here are two quick lamb preparations that you can serve in place of the kebabs. Each recipe serves two, but can double easily; both partner well with the pilaf and the romaine salad.

RACK OF LAMB

A "frenched" rack of lamb has had the chine bone removed by the butcher, making it easier to carve. The butcher will also trim the rib bones by about two inches, leaving the ends of the bones exposed and the rib-eye of meat intact. Tying two racks together produces the aptly-named crown roast of lamb.

1 tablespoon olive oil
1 tablespoon coarse or kosher salt
2 teaspoons coarsely ground black pepper
1 rack of lamb, about 1¼ lb., "frenched"

1. Preheat the oven to 450°F. Make a paste of the oil, salt, and pepper and rub on all sides of the lamb rib-eye. Cover the bones with foil to prevent them from blackening in the hot oven. Place the rack of lamb on a heavy-gauge sheet pan and roast for 10 minutes.

2. Lower the heat to 350°F and roast until the lamb is medium-rare (internal temperature of 130°F), another 15 to 20 minutes.

SERVES 2

OVEN-ROASTED LAMB CHOPS

Loin lamb chops have a fragile little T-bone and a more delicate flavor than rib chops. Look for meat that is a fairly light red and finely textured (not grainy), with bones that look moist and reddish.

> 4 loin lamb chops, cut 2 inches thick (about 1³/₄ lb.)
> 2 garlic cloves, peeled and smashed
> 2 teaspoons coarse or kosher salt
> 1 teaspoon coarsely ground black pepper
> About 2 tablespoons olive oil

1. Preheat the oven to 350°F. Rub both sides of the lamb chops with garlic, salt, and pepper and set aside.

2. Lightly film a heavy ovenproof skillet with oil and wipe out the excess with a paper towel. (There's no need to leave a pool of oil in the pan, as the fat on the meat will render while the lamb cooks, keeping the chops from sticking.) Heat the skillet over medium-high heat until almost smoking; the oil will start to shimmer and glisten, and it will appear to pucker. Sear the lamb chops until browned (about 2 minutes on each side) and immediately transfer the skillet to the oven.

3. Roast the chops 10 minutes for rare; medium-rare will take about 12 minutes. Testing for doneness is by trial and error: Use the tip of a sharp paring knife to make a small slit in the center of a chop and peek inside, bearing in mind that the chops will continue cooking after you remove them from the oven.

SERVES 2

Party Food

1 Smoky Chili with Toppings, Rice with Orzo, Sort-of-Salad

2 Beef Bourguignon, Rice with Orzo, Roasted Carrots with Garlic

3 Sausage and Mushroom Lasagna *or* Wild Mushroom Lasagna, Grilled Zucchini

4 Chicken Breasts with Honey and Herbs, Nutted Wheat Pilaf, Asparagus and Portobello Salad *or* Chicken Breasts with Honey and Herbs, Grilled Endive,Radicchio, and Red Onion, Basil-Grilled Cherry Tomatoes

5 Southwestern Pork Tenderloin, Twice-baked Potatoes, Skillet Slaw

3

Party Food

Meals for Six and More

Party food differs from dining *à deux*. Unlike individually portioned dishes (like lamb chops), one-dish meals make ideal party fare because they're flexible enough to handle a last-minute addition to your guest list (maybe even two).

The best party foods are tried-and-true favorites. No matter how adventurous your own palate, this isn't the time to initiate anyone into the world of weird cuisine.

To think beyond table seating and into the world of buffet entertaining, you must: (1) Forget magazine photographs featuring farmhouse tables laden with dozens of hubcap-sized bowls and platters. What makes a buffet isn't an extravaganza of food; it simply means that the meal is set out on a table, sideboard, or kitchen island. (2) Stop obsessing about where guests will sit. Trust them to make themselves comfortable—eating standing up, or sitting wherever they find space and balancing plates on their laps. Although a buffet may seem awkward at first, once it gets going, it offers guests the ultimate luxury: freedom to choose their dinner companions and change them at will.

For the new host, entertaining in the buffet style can be very liberating: Six quickly becomes eight, and before you know it, there are twelve. Now you are on your way to becoming a bona fide *bon vivant*.

1/Smoky Chili with Toppings *or* Beef Bourguignon with Roasted Carrots and Garlic
> Rice with Orzo
> Sort-of-Salad

It might seem a shame that without a wedding to my name, I've never benefited from the booty that comes along with being a bride. However, after dating for decades, I have been the frequently delighted, sometimes baffled recipient of many gifts from men—gifts ranging from the wifely-cozy (tea kettles and bathrobes) and frilly-girly (bath salts and little silk pillows) to the just plain horrible (for Christmas, my awful old boyfriend the wannabe fashion photographer gave me a picture he had taken of another woman—both the gift and the girl were "unwrapped").

Without a doubt, the best gift I've ever gotten was from a man who enrolled me in a bacon-of-the-month club. And since he was also that club's founder, the right word from him got me the whole year's supply in a single overnight delivery. After lovingly storing a dozen of America's best bacons in my refrigerator, I kept the cardboard packing box on my kitchen counter for days. Every so often I'd unfold the top and stick my head inside for a deep whiff. It wasn't just the sugar-cured, hickory-smoked aroma that made me swoon—that box smelled like fat.

For the next few months there was bacon in or on top of everything I cooked. Then I discovered that the best place to put bacon is *under* food, lacing any dish with deeply penetrating smokiness. You can bet there's bacon at the bottom of this chili. Buy the best bacon you can find and cook it slowly until it gives up its fat. Then saturate the onions with the bacon drippings, making sure to follow the recipe and take five full minutes to cook the spices into a rich paste that gives a

THE BEST BACON

If you're talking to me, you can't just claim to love bacon. I need to believe that you love it for all the right reasons: the saltiness that keeps you thirsty no matter how much you drink, the smokiness on your fingertips that leaves you smelling like someone in a Walker Evans photograph, that penetrating aroma of warm fat hanging in the air like a shroud. As far as I'm concerned, there is no such thing as bad bacon. But there is such a thing as better bacon (called boutique or artisanal bacon), and it is well worth the time and trouble it might take to find it.

Unlike factory-made bacon, mass-produced to please our homogenized, everybody-in-khaki national palate, boutique bacons made at smaller smokehouses are crafted to very specific, very individualized styles, with distinct flavorings, regional characteristics, and varying degrees of salt and smoke. In the Northeast, maple syrup may be used as a cure ingredient; in the South, brown sugar. Boutique bacons are smoked over hickory wood in some states, corncobs in others.

If taste isn't enough to motivate you, what about shrinkage? When the bacon producers, geared toward supplying every supermarket in America, speed up the smoking process by using shortcuts like liquid smoke, you know what happens: You start out with a pan full of promise and end up with crispy shards of twisted meat. Boutique brands won't disappear in your pan, because they've been smoked over real wood long enough (or at a temperature high enough) to render much of the fat while the bacon is still in the smokehouse. A great bacon is also sliced thick enough to sink your teeth into. "We grew up in the country," says Khoury Mubarek of Nodine's Smokehouse in Torrington, Connecticut (one of the country's finest boutique brands). "We don't think you should be able to read a newspaper through a slice of our bacon."

For most of us, boutique bacon is once-in-a-while bacon, not because of how we live but where we live. Without national distributors—which very few small smokehouses have—locally made bacons are mostly confined to their own little corner of the country. But since you're not the only bacon lover in town, I guarantee you that somewhere in your area there's a specialty-food shop bringing in selections from regional smokehouses. Track those places down and support them. (You can also try the better butcher shops.)

If that fails, you've still got Internet research and mail order. Many smokehouses will ship straight to you, but I'll warn you: It's not cheap. Not only are there overnight shipping costs, there is often a 5- or 6-pound minimum. But going out of your way to find good bacon is not about being a snob or fetishizing an everyday grocery-store purchase. Sure, it might be about taste, but it's also about value.

beautiful sheen to the finished chili. Do that and you'll soon realize that bacon is the gift that keeps on giving.

Stacking Textures

I learned almost everything I know about chili from the late Michael McLaughlin, a former restaurateur and food writer who devoted a significant part of his thirty-year career to deconstructing and (lucky for me) constructing chili. In addition to making sure I understood the need for pure unseasoned chili powder (grocery store blends contain dehydrated onions, garlic, and a bevy of other flavorings you don't want) and the secret step of sprinkling in some cornmeal near the end of cooking time (to absorb the fat), Michael taught me that cooking the spices in order to deepen the color and flavor makes a big difference in the way chili looks and, of course, tastes.

It doesn't take much to understand that the rice and orzo is intended as a base, soaking up the sauce and cutting through the slickness of this deep, intense chili. But this two-grain combo is a far cry from standard steamed white rice; it has seasonings similar to those of the chili, but enough separate flavor identity to stand alone.

Although serving a salad on a buffet often strikes the new (or lazy) host as a good (read "easy") way to round out a plate, leafy lettuce is

hard to eat while standing, and in this case, when the cool vinaigrette meets the hot chili, the result is a sloppy mess of wilted greens. Instead, let each guest choose from a variety of salad separates to provide crispness and crunch, not to mention color and flavor. Dessert: Play up that classic Mexican *mole* pairing of chocolate and chilies—serve Chocolate Espresso Bourbon Cake (page 155), plated with brown sugar-and-vanilla whipped cream, or cut into bite-sized brownies and served with *dulce de leche* ice cream.

Social Scenario

Relax: This is not being offered as the definitive chili recipe. There's no need for any chili-head arguments over rice/no rice; beans/no beans. The goal here is to feed many different kinds of people at the same time, and chili is simply excellent party food—adaptable, low key, and easy to "stretch" to serve more guests. Plus, this is one of those rare times when you can actually please all of the people: The toppings, assorted by the whim of each guest, turn every plate into a singular interpretation. So invite a crowd. Even a vegetarian—if you have occasion to invite such a creature into your home—can skip the chili and turn the toppings into a main-course salad.

TOPPING IT OFF

Chili is more fun for a party when you dress it up. Try some—or all—of these toppers and accompaniments.

BREAD
- Cornbread
- Sourdough rolls
- Flour tortillas
- Chowder crackers
- Cheddar Cheese Shortbread (page 31)

CHEESE
- Grated Vella Jack
- Shredded Monterey Jack, plain or peppered
- Shredded orange or yellow Cheddar
- Soft goat cheese, plain or herbed

SOUR CREAM
- Plain sour cream
- Chipotle Sour Cream (page 125)

SALSA
Anything from *tradicionál* to *nuevo:*
- salsa fresca
- salsa verde
- pico de gallo
- roasted corn/tomato
- mango/tomatillo

SMOKY CHILI

A few lessons: Chipotle chili powder provides the heat, so depending on your own thermostat, use less or more. Your butcher has different-size grinding disks and may be willing to grind your beef through the coarsest one; it will make a chunkier chili. Finally, don't ruin good chili with discount beans. Sample different brands until you find beans that are shiny and firm. The best brand I've found is S&W, available in supermarkets. Don't buy pre-chopped green chilies; they don't retain enough of their oils.

½ lb. smoky bacon (slab bacon, diced,or thickly sliced bacon, chopped)
3 large yellow onions, peeled and chopped (about 3 cups)
2 lb. coarsely ground beef (chuck)
2 lb. coarsely ground pork (shoulder)
About 2 teaspoons coarse or kosher salt
⅓ cup mild unseasoned chili powder, or to taste
3 tablespoons ground cumin
3 tablespoons Mexican oregano
2 tablespoons chipotle chili powder
2 tablespoons ground cinnamon
1½ cups canned Italian tomatoes, crushed by hand, with their juices
6 cups superior beef stock
6 cloves garlic, finely chopped
3 whole canned green chilies, finely chopped
Ground black pepper to taste
2 (15-oz.) cans red kidney beans, rinsed under gently running cool water and drained
¼ cup apple cider vinegar
1 tablespoon yellow cornmeal

1. Place the bacon in a medium stockpot (at least 8 quarts) over medium-low heat and cook until the bacon renders its fat, 5 to 8 minutes. Remove the bacon with a slotted spoon (leaving as much of the drippings behind as possible) and reserve for use in the rice recipe. Raise the heat to medium and add the onions, stirring to coat. Cook until the onions are soft and the edges begin to color, 12 to 15 minutes. Remove to a separate bowl.

2. Working in small batches, add the beef and pork, sprinkle with salt, and cook until both meats lose their pink color, 18 to 20 minutes. (At this point the meat does not have to be cooked all the way through.) Return the onions to the stockpot and stir to combine. Add the unseasoned chili powder and the other spices and cook, stirring constantly, until everything is well coated and the mixture is a deep mahogany color, about 5 minutes.

3. Add the tomatoes and stock, stirring well to scrape up any browned onions and meat from the bottom of the pot. Bring the mixture to a boil. Lower the heat and simmer uncovered, stirring occasionally, until the chili thickens, about 1 hour. Stir in the garlic and green chilies, and continue to simmer for another 30 minutes. Taste for seasoning, adding pepper and more salt (if needed). The recipe can be prepared in advance up to this point.

4. Just before serving, toss the beans with the vinegar. Add them to the chili and simmer for another 5 minutes. Stir in the cornmeal and serve.

SERVES 6

RICE WITH ORZO

Enhancing ordinary rice with orzo (grain-shaped pasta) and shallots adds another taste and texture dimension. This dish also goes with Beef Bourguignon (page 92). Add the jalapeño if you're serving chili, orange zest if you're going with the beef.

> 5 tablespoons unsalted butter
> ½ cup orzo
> 2 cups long-grain white rice
> 3½ cups superior beef stock mixed with 1 cup water
> 1 tablespoon olive oil
> 3 shallots, finely chopped
> 1 tablespoon finely chopped jalapeño (for chili)
>   or minced orange zest (for bourguignon)

1. In a small stockpot with a tight-fitting lid, melt 4 tablespoons of butter over low heat. Add the orzo and cook, stirring frequently, until lightly toasted, about 3 minutes. Add the rice, stirring to coat each grain with melted butter. Raise the heat to medium-high, add the stock and water, and bring to a boil. Lower the heat, cover, and simmer until the rice is cooked and the liquid has been absorbed.

2. While the rice is cooking, in a small skillet over medium-high heat melt the remaining 1 tablespoon butter with the oil until foamy. Add the shallots and jalapeño (if serving with chili) and cook, stirring occasionally, until lightly browned, 3 to 5 minutes. Stir this mixture into the rice. If serving with beef bourguignon, stir in the orange zest.

SERVES 6

SORT-OF-SALAD

Think of these as salad separates, and serve them in individual bowls so your guests can mix and match them into any combination they like. If you've cooked up a double batch of chili for a large crowd, be sure to double to salad quantities, too.

2 avocados, diced
1 large red onion, coarsely chopped
1 large white onion, coarsely chopped
1 small bunch (about 4) green onions, chopped
2 large ripe red tomatoes
2 large ripe yellow tomatoes, coarsely chopped
1 small head romaine, shredded
½ cup pickled jalapeños, diced
2 cups salsa

SERVES 6

2/Beef Bourguignon
➤ Roasted Carrots with Garlic
➤ Rice with Orzo

Social Scenario

Beef bourguignon and chili share the same buffet-party sensibilities: They are easy to eat without a knife, and almost everyone likes them (although bourguignon may be the uptown version). And you can make either dish a day in advance to minimize party-day cooking.

Stacking Textures

As in the chili, the beef in the bourguignon is browned and then tenderized by slow cooking in the oven that marries the other ingredients into a rich sauce (served over rice). Traditional beef bourguignon includes pearl onions and carrots, but this time, the onions have been replaced by shallots, and the carrots are oven-roasted to bring out their natural sweetness and served as a side dish. Dessert: No question—hot apple crisp (page 158). It's tarte Tatin for the less talented.

GIVING GOOD HOST: SETTING UP THE BUFFET

Let's say you've decided to double (or even triple) the chili recipe and are now about to face what feels like a Super Bowl stadium full of guests. When it comes to setting up your place for a big buffet, you might think you're creating more room by pushing your table against a wall. But when you do, the table acts like a dam, impeding the free flow of guests and causing an even bigger traffic jam. It is better to position the table with access from both sides, creating a double buffet line. Placing food platters on both sides also produces a more sociable atmosphere, letting guests talk across the table while they get their food.

Before the party, assemble the serving platters and bowls (as well as serving utensils) to make sure that every dish on the menu will have a home. Write down the name of each dish on a sticky note and attach it to the appropriate serving piece so you'll remember what goes where: What seems elementary now will be essential when you are distracted by guests and alcohol.

BEEF BOURGUIGNON

Combining port and brandy with the usual red wine adds richness, depth, and just a touch of sweetness to the sauce.

½ teaspoon whole black peppercorns
2 stems fresh thyme
1 bay leaf
¼ cup vegetable oil
4 cloves garlic, peeled and smashed
3½ lb. trimmed beef chuck, cut into 1½-inch cubes and patted dry with paper towels
⅓ cup flour
2 teaspoons coarse or kosher salt
1 teaspoon ground black pepper
¼ cup Cognac
½ cup ruby port
2½ cups dry red wine, such as Burgundy
1 tablespoon tomato paste whisked into 1½ cups superior beef stock
1 tablespoon unsalted butter
2 tablespoons olive oil
2 shallots, finely chopped
1 lb. small mushrooms (as uniform as possible), cleaned and trimmed

1. Preheat the oven to 350°F. Place the peppercorns, thyme and bay leaf in a spice bag (see page 48) but do not tie it closed; set aside.

2. Heat the oil in a heavy ovenproof casserole (see page 49) over medium heat. Add the garlic and cook until lightly colored, about 3 minutes. Remove the garlic cloves and add them to the spice bag.

3. Raise the heat to medium-high. Working in small batches and keeping the meat in one layer, brown the beef on all sides in the flavored oil—a messy but necessary step that adds to the richness of the finished dish. Return all the meat to the casserole and sprinkle evenly with flour, salt, and pepper. Reduce the heat and cook, stirring frequently, until the meat is evenly browned and well coated.

4. Heat the Cognac in a small saucepan over low heat until warm, about 1 minute. Tilt the pan to pool the Cognac in one side and, holding a long kitchen match at arm's length, ignite the alcohol fumes. Pour the still-flaming Cognac over the beef. When the flames die down, add the port, red wine, the stock mixture, and the spice bag, and bring to a boil. Cover the casserole and place on the center rack in the oven. Cook until the meat is tender, about 2 hours.

5. Carefully remove the casserole from the oven and place on a burner over low heat. Simmer uncovered for about 15 minutes to thicken the sauce.

Meanwhile, in a heavy skillet over medium-high heat melt the butter with the oil until foamy. Brown the shallots in the skillet, then add the mushrooms and cook, stirring occasionally, until golden, about 5 minutes. Stir the mushrooms and shallots into the casserole.

SERVES 6

ROASTED CARROTS WITH GARLIC

For best flavor, buy loose carrots, not bagged. About five largish carrots should weigh 2½ pounds. The carrots must be roasted in batches because you can't put them all on the baking sheet at once—overcrowding will cause them to steam instead of roasting.

    12 large cloves garlic, peeled and halved
    About 3 tablespoons olive oil
    2½ lb. carrots, peeled and trimmed
    Coarse or kosher salt and ground black pepper
    2 tablespoons finely chopped flat-leaf parsley

1. Preheat the oven to 450°F. Line a heavy-gauge sheet pan with cooking parchment (see page 30) or spray lightly with nonstick cooking spray, wiping off the excess with a paper towel.

2. Place the garlic cloves in a small bowl, add about 1 teaspoon of oil, and toss until well coated but not dripping; set aside.

3. Cut the carrots on a long diagonal into ⅓-inch-thick slices about 2 inches long. Place the carrots in a large mixing bowl and toss with the remaining oil until well-coated but not dripping. Lightly sprinkle with salt and pepper (you can always add more later) and toss.

4. Arrange the carrots in a single layer in the pan; there should be space around each slice. Roast the first batch of carrots until brown on the edges, about 8 minutes. Using a spatula, turn the carrots and continue roasting 3 to 5 minutes longer. Slide the pan out of the oven and, working quickly, sprinkle some of the garlic over the carrots and mix with a spatula. Return the pan to the oven and roast until the carrots are crisp-tender and the garlic is browned, another 3 to 5 minutes. Transfer the cooked carrots to a serving bowl and then cook the remaining carrots. Salt and pepper to taste; sprinkle with parsley.

SERVES 6

93

3/Sausage and Mushroom Lasagna *or* Wild Mushroom Lasagna
➤ Grilled Zucchini

After twenty years spent submerged in New York's changing restaurant scene, I know one thing for sure: the city that never sleeps can't keep its mouth shut, either. It's not just the volume. Crowds and cramped tables guarantee that by the end of any evening, I will know too much about something I shouldn't know at all.

Sometimes, in order to have a good meal and keep my conversation private, it's easier to stay at home and cook. Especially on weekends. Although it may not compete with the nightlife most out-of-towners have in mind when they fantasize about moving to New York, I am able to lure true urbanites by offering them a quiet evening. Then I promise to coddle them with something simple, something cozy— something with a lot of melted cheese.

You'd be surprised at how effective my invitation is during the late fall, when Sunday nights take on that weird school-night sadness—no matter how old you are. Everyone seems to want a little culinary reassurance, the kind of food they don't have to figure out how to eat. I try to make something that tastes familiar without being boring, like this updated version of that old school-cafeteria classic. When it comes time to eat, we pass the plates around in silent agreement: It's not comfort food unless you're comfortable.

Stacking Textures

Heavy cream, ricotta and two cups of the best Parmigiano-Reggiano: obviously a meal just crying out for something green. But don't be a slave to salad. Unlike lettuce, grilled zucchini won't suffer (or get soggy) when drenched with sauce (since zucchini are rather bland, the flavor will actually be improved). Dessert: poached oranges (page 153) accompanied by chocolate truffles (see "How to Buy Truffles," page 169).

Social Scenario

There is no way to equate the sort of entertaining that goes on in restaurants with the easy informality of a party in your own home. Take advantage of the intimacy by inviting not only people you already know, but those you would like to get to know. Although it takes a heap of man-hours to make lasagna, it isn't the kind of work people have to witness. Since you can make the lasagna the day before (and grill the zucchini hours before guests arrive), this menu is tailor-made for a party when you actually want to spend time with your guests.

Cooking Strategy

Like most good party food, lasagna is a make-it-the-day-before dish that doesn't need any last-minute preparation or split-second timing; it doesn't even need to be served piping hot (which means it can survive on a buffet table). Now that I've passed on the good news about lasagna, let me bare the bad: making lasagna is boring and not all that cheap (at least this one isn't).

Lasagna is a real labor-of-love meal, and certainly nothing for a host to enter into, or offer to others, lightly. Cooking the noodles until tender but still firm, draining and drying them is a time-consuming job. The noodles must separate without sticking or tearing and be easy to handle when you are layering the lasagna.

If you do opt to make the lasagna a day ahead, know this: Successfully reheating an entire pan of lasagna is an almost impossible task, because the edges burn before the center is warm enough. Instead, cut cold lasagna into individual serving portions, transfer to a sheet pan, and bring to room temperature. Bake in a preheated 350°F oven until warmed through, 8 to 10 minutes. Bonus: When you reheat lasagna this way, each piece gets those crispy little edges that everyone loves. It helps to use a small offset spatula (one with a right-angle dip in the handle and a thin, flexible "tongue" that will easily slide under the portions of lasagna) to make the trip from baking sheet to serving plate fast and neat.

SAUSAGE AND MUSHROOM LASAGNA

The lasagna-making process can be divided into two stages: Preparation (steps 1 through 4) and Assembly/Cooking (steps 5 through 7). Your favorite supermarket brand of tomato sauce will work fine here as long as it is relatively smooth and not too spicy. For a better-tasting, better-looking lasagna, be sure to cook the mushrooms in small batches so they'll get brown and slightly crisp. If the skillet is crowded, they'll just steam and soften.

2 lb. sweet Italian sausage
10 oz. dry lasagna noodles
About ¹⁄₂ cup olive oil
2 lb. portobello mushroom caps
¹⁄₂ lb. large white mushrooms
¹⁄₄ cup finely chopped flat-leaf parsley
Coarse or kosher salt and ground black pepper (amounts depend on the
    spiciness of the sausage and sauce you use)
2 cups hand-grated Parmigiano-Reggiano
1¹⁄₂ cups ricotta
1¹⁄₂ cups heavy cream
5 cups tomato sauce

1. Preheat the oven to 350°F. Remove the sausage from its casings and place in a shallow roasting pan or sheet pan. Cook the sausage in the oven until thoroughly cooked and no longer pink, 20 to 25 minutes. Drain the cooking liquid from the pan, cool the sausage until easy to handle, and crumble it into a bowl.

2. (If you are using no-boil noodles, skip steps 2 and 3.) Fill a medium

THE EQUIPMENT: OVENPROOF BAKING DISH
Since this is a party dish, skip the standard 13 x 9-inch lasagna pan (which only serves 6 to 8) and opt for a 15 x 10-inch ovenproof glass baking dish, which serves 10 to 12, conducts heat well, and cleans up easily. If you're tempted to use a disposable foil baking tin, don't. Foil can never get hot enough to thoroughly cook this filling, and the end result, after all your best intentions, will be more like soup than lasagna.

An acceptable shortcut, whether you are making several pans of lasagna or just one in a hurry: no-boil noodles. Thicker and not as tender as dry pasta (that you cook), no-boil lasagna noodles are available at specialty food stores and many large supermarkets. For best quality, buy a brand made in Italy. Since Italian noodles absorb liquid (and expand) while cooking, soak them in boiling water for about 20 minutes before using to plump them up (don't stack them because they will stick together), and layer them in the lasagna so they are close but not overlapping.

mixing bowl with several trays of ice cubes, at least 2 cups cold water, and 2 tablespoons of oil; set aside. Line a sheet pan with a clean, damp kitchen towel and have several others available. (A dry towel will stick.)

3. In a large stockpot of abundantly salted boiling water, cook the lasagna noodles (only 3 or 4 at a time) until al dente, about 4 minutes. Using a slotted spoon or mesh sieve (tongs will tear the noodles), immediately transfer the noodles to the ice bath to stop the cooking process. When the noodles are cool, remove them, drain thoroughly, and spread them on the dampened towels. Repeat, putting a dampened towel between each layer of noodles.

4. Clean and trim the mushrooms, cutting the portobello caps into $\frac{1}{2}$-inch cubes and slicing the white mushroom caps thinly. (At this point, keep the mushrooms separate.) In a large skillet over medium-high heat, heat 3 tablespoons of oil until hot but not smoking (a drop of water should sizzle immediately upon contact). Cook the portobellos in small batches, stirring, until golden brown (5 to 7 minutes), transferring each cooked batch to a large bowl. Use the same technique to cook the white mushrooms, then add them to the mixing bowl. Sprinkle the mushrooms with half the parsley, then season with salt and pepper; toss to combine and set aside to cool.

5. Preheat the oven to 350°F. Lightly brush the bottom and sides of a 15 x 10-inch ovenproof glass baking dish with oil. Mix 2 tablespoons of the grated cheese with 1 tablespoon of the remaining parsley. Combine the ricotta with the cream. In a small bowl, mix $\frac{1}{4}$ cup of the tomato sauce with $\frac{1}{4}$ cup of the ricotta mixture and set aside.

6. Place a layer of noodles in the bottom of the baking dish. Cover the noodles with about one-third each of the mushrooms, sausage, sauce, ricotta mixture, grated cheese, and parsley. Sprinkle with salt and pepper. Add two more layers, finishing with a top layer of noodles. Spread the reserved sauce and ricotta mixture over the top and sprinkle with the grated cheese-parsley mixture.

7. Cover the dish tightly with foil and bake the lasagna until the edges are bubbly, 30 to 40 minutes. Remove the foil and bake until the top is lightly browned and crisp, 10 to 15 minutes longer. You can also place the pan under a preheated broiler for about 2 minutes to give the top of the lasagna a good crisping. Let the lasagna stand for 10 or 15 minutes before serving.

SERVES 8

GRILLED ZUCCHINI

The success of this dish lies in the shopping. Oversized zucchini can be watery and filled with seeds, so look for the smaller versions with thin, smooth, glossy skin. When you press the zucchini with your thumb, it should feel firm right down to the ends.

8 small, unblemished zucchini (as uniform as possible), about 2½ lb.
About 3 tablespoons olive oil
Coarse or kosher salt
Ground black pepper

1. Trim the ends, then halve the zucchini lengthwise. Resting each half on its cut side, pare a long, thin strip of skin lengthwise from each piece (this helps it brown on both sides). Lightly brush both sides of each piece with oil.

2. Film a grill pan (see page 104) or heavy skillet with oil and heat over high heat until almost smoking: The pan must be hot enough to sear the zucchini on contact. Cook the zucchini in small batches (do not overcrowd the pan), cut-side down, until browned and slightly crisp, about 3 minutes. Turn to brown the other side, about 2 minutes longer. Transfer to a serving platter and sprinkle with salt and pepper.

SERVES 8

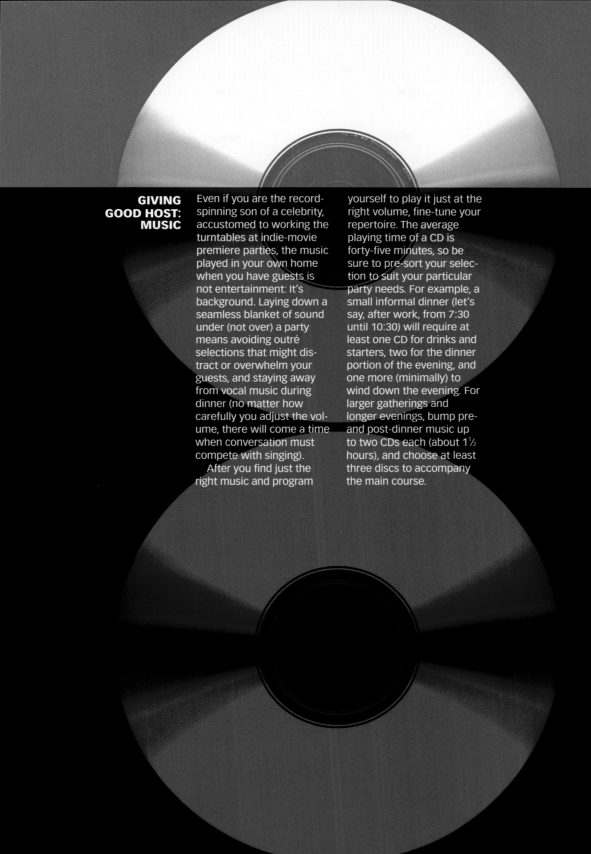

GIVING GOOD HOST: MUSIC

Even if you are the record-spinning son of a celebrity, accustomed to working the turntables at indie-movie premiere parties, the music played in your own home when you have guests is not entertainment: It's background. Laying down a seamless blanket of sound under (not over) a party means avoiding outré selections that might distract or overwhelm your guests, and staying away from vocal music during dinner (no matter how carefully you adjust the volume, there will come a time when conversation must compete with singing).

After you find just the right music and program yourself to play it just at the right volume, fine-tune your repertoire. The average playing time of a CD is forty-five minutes, so be sure to pre-sort your selection to suit your particular party needs. For example, a small informal dinner (let's say, after work, from 7:30 until 10:30) will require at least one CD for drinks and starters, two for the dinner portion of the evening, and one more (minimally) to wind down the evening. For larger gatherings and longer evenings, bump pre- and post-dinner music up to two CDs each (about 1½ hours), and choose at least three discs to accompany the main course.

WILD MUSHROOM LASAGNA

This slightly more sophisticated variation is made in a standard 13 x 9-inch lasagna pan. It has the same instant béchamel-style sauce between the layers as the other recipe, and is hearty enough to satisfy both the vegetarians and the not-so-vegetarians. However, you might also choose to serve a platter of grilled sausages on the side.

4 ounces dried porcini mushrooms
4 cups tomato sauce
About ½ cup olive oil
8 oz. dry lasagna noodles
1½ lb. portobello mushrooms
½ lb. large white mushrooms
Coarse or kosher salt
Ground black pepper
1½ cups hand-grated Parmigiano-Reggiano
¼ cup finely chopped flat-leaf parsley
1⅓ cups ricotta
1⅓ cups heavy cream

1. Place the porcini in a bowl and cover with 2 cups of boiling water. Let soak until softened, at least 30 minutes. Remove the porcini with a slotted spoon and strain the liquid through a double thickness of cheesecloth. (You should have about ½ cup.) In a small saucepan over medium-high heat, reduce the liquid to ¼ cup. Add to the tomato sauce and set aside. Finely chop the softened porcini and reserve. (You can do this in a small food processor fited with a metal blade as long as you don't pulverize them.)

2. (If you are using no-boil noodles, skip steps 2 and 3.) Fill a medium mixing bowl with several trays of ice cubes, at least 2 cups cold water, and 2 tablespoons of oil; set aside. Line a sheet pan with a clean, damp kitchen towel and have several others available.

3. In a large stockpot of abundantly salted boiling water, cook the lasagna noodles (only 3 or 4 at a time) until al dente, about 4 minutes. Using a slotted spoon or mesh sieve (tongs will tear the noodles), immediately transfer the noodles to the ice bath to stop the cooking process. When the noodles are cool, remove them, drain thoroughly, and spread them on the dampened towels. Repeat, putting a dampened towel between each layer of noodles.

4. Clean and trim the mushrooms, cutting the portobello caps into ½-inch cubes and slicing the white mushroom caps thinly. (At this point, keep the mushrooms separate.) In a large skillet over medium-high heat, heat 3 table-spoons of oil until hot but not smoking (a drop of water should sizzle immediately upon contact). Cook the portobellos in small batches, stirring, until golden brown (5 to 7 minutes), transferring each cooked batch to a large bowl. Use the same technique to cook the white mushrooms, then add them to the bowl. Season with salt and pepper and toss to combine; set aside to cool.

5. Preheat the oven to 350°F. Lightly brush the bottom and sides of a 13 x 9-inch ovenproof glass baking dish with oil. Mix 2 tablespoons of the grated cheese with 1 tablespoon of the parsley. Combine the ricotta with the cream. In a small bowl, mix about ¼ cup of tomato sauce with ¼ cup of the ricotta mixture and set aside.

6. Place a layer of noodles in the bottom of the baking dish. Cover the noodles with about one-third each of the mushrooms, sauce, ricotta mixture, grated cheese, and parsley. Sprinkle with pepper. Add two more layers, finishing with a top layer of noodles. Spread the reserved sauce and ricotta mixture over the top and sprinkle with the cheese-parsley mixture.

7. Cover the dish tightly with foil and bake the lasagna until the edges are bubbly, 30 to 40 minutes. Remove the foil and bake until the top is lightly browned and crisp, 10 to 15 minutes longer. Allow the lasagna to stand for 10 to 15 minutes before serving.

SERVES 6

4/Chicken Breasts with Honey and Herbs
➤ Nutted Wheat Pilaf
➤ Asparagus and Portobello Salad

I can't reveal exactly when or where I catered a big dinner for the Vice President of the United States. Suffice it to say we were both there for the money. Although you might assume that preparing a buffet for a group of hobnobbers is different from entertaining a bunch of your own friends, let me assure you that with the exception of Dusty the bomb-sniffing dog, a Swat Team of sharpshooters stationed on the roof, and the two dozen (strangely sexy) Secret Service guys sporting ear wires and handguns, it's pretty much the same. You want a meal that can feed the maximum number of people while requiring the minimum amount of time in the kitchen before and during the party—dishes with flexible timing, designed to look good and taste good at room temperature (in the event your guests are held up by some sort of national security crisis).

For this specific political party, I also had to consider dictates of protocol: no veal (too issue-oriented); no lamb (objectionable when served at room temperature); no beef (hostess wouldn't allow red wine in the living room); and absolutely no fish (shell or otherwise). I was pretty much limited to the original white meat, but despite the jokes you're dying to make, this was no replay of the time-honored rubber-chicken dinner. The chicken breasts were seared in a grill pan on top of the stove and finished in a hot oven, emerging beautifully browned and succulent. As a matter of fact, one of the waiters reported that several guests wanted to know my trick for keeping the chicken breasts so tender and juicy. "Can I give them the recipe," I asked the Secret Service agent standing guard in the kitchen, "if I leave out all the gore-y details?"

Stacking Textures

What's important about the texture of buffet food is staying power: the texture should not change as the dishes sit at room temperature. This chicken will remain juicy and not dry out (even though it is pre-sliced for serving ease); the wheat pilaf (more manageable than potatoes if guests are standing) will continue to hold the flavor of the citrus dressing without getting soggy, and the earthy asparagus and mushroom combination will stay crisp-tender (there is no vinaigrette to soften the vegetables or dull their color). If you opt for the outdoor version of this meal (see pages 108–109), you'll initially be dishing up the vegetables hot off the grill, but they'll be in good shape to serve as seconds even after they've cooled to room temperature. Dessert: in cool weather, apple or pear crisp (page 158), right out of the oven, with vanilla ice cream and butterscotch sauce (page 166). In warmer months, cold plum or peach crisp with brown-sugar-and-vanilla whipped cream (page 165).

Social Scenario

When you want to keep it simple enough that you can enjoy your own party, but sophisticated enough that your guests are impressed—even if they're busy running for President.

Cooking Strategy

These chicken breasts will taste better if you cook them close enough to party time that they won't need refrigeration (about two hours). For a buffet, slice each chicken breast lengthwise into long strips and then reassemble the breast, arranging them toward the center of an oval serving platter. (This way your guests will be able to handle the chicken with just a fork.) Since a platter of chicken breasts (no matter how well prepared) can look boring, tuck lemon rounds and sprigs of fresh herbs here and there between the chicken slices, and place some asparagus and portobello salad at either end of the dish.

CHICKEN BREASTS WITH HONEY AND HERBS

Let me give you a little tip about chicken: Buying it on sale is no bargain. Don't super-market it. Buy the best you can. Get boneless skinless breasts, all roughly the same size (¾ to 1 lb. each) from a good butcher, and ask him to cut them in half for you. Rinse the chicken under cool running water and pat dry with paper towels before slipping it into the marinade. Choose a honey that is not too sweet, more earthy than flowery, like chestnut or wild thyme honey.

> 4 boneless, skinless double chicken breasts, halved (8 pieces, about 3½ lb. total weight)
> ½ cup fresh lemon juice
> ½ cup white wine
> About 2 tablespoons olive oil
> 2 teaspoons honey
> 2 tablespoons minced lemon zest
> 2 tablespoons finely chopped flat-leaf parsley
> 2 tablespoons finely chopped fresh thyme (or rosemary)
> 2 tablespoons snipped fresh chives
> ½ teaspoon kosher salt
> ½ teaspoon cracked black pepper

1. Place the chicken breasts in a large glass, ceramic, or stainless-steel bowl and set aside. Combine all the remaining ingredients and pour over the chicken, turning to coat each breast. Marinate for at least 4 hours.

THE EQUIPMENT: GRILL PANS
Stovetop grill pans have parallel ridges (like speed bumps) across the bottom to lift the food slightly so it isn't sitting in fat while it cooks. Those ridges also "mark" it, making those picture-perfect grill imprints that magazine food stylists love. I prefer a small, lightweight, square nonstick grill pan to the heavy cast-iron variety. But when it comes to kitchen equipment, no one can tell you exactly what to buy without knowing your stove—intimately. My only suggestion is that you choose a pan that fits your burners and conducts heat well.

When you're feeding a crowd for lunch, the breasts can be thinly sliced and layered with slow-roasted tomatoes (page 29) and crisp romaine lettuce on sourdough bread to make two-handed chicken sandwiches. Or, you can shred the chicken and toss it with blanched green beans, cherry tomatoes, and tiny roasted new potatoes for a grilled chicken salad.

2. Preheat the oven to 350°F. Drain and discard the marinade and pat the chicken dry with paper towels. It is important that the chicken breasts be dry before you grill them, or they will steam instead of searing.

3. Place a grill pan over high heat. Lightly film the bottom of the pan with olive oil, using paper towels to wipe out any excess. Heat the pan until hot but not smoking; the chicken should sear instantly when it hits the pan. Working two at a time, place the chicken breasts in the pan and sear until golden-brown grill marks appear, about 2 minutes. (Try not to move the chicken breasts while they are being "marked.") Turn the breasts and mark the other side (this will take less time). Transfer to a heavy-gauge sheet pan.

4. Place the pan in the oven and roast until the breasts are cooked through (no longer pink inside), 10 to 12 minutes. Bear in mind that the chicken will continue to cook after you take it out of the oven. Transfer the pan to a rack and cool to room temperature.

SERVES 6 TO 8

NUTTED WHEAT PILAF

I worked for several years at The Silver Palate, New York City's famous food store, where this salad was a catering staple. Over the years, I used it in my own catering business, continually adapting the recipe to reflect changing tastes. It takes several hours for the pilaf to cool and dry, so you might want to cook it the night before; do not, however, refrigerate it. The wheat pilaf mix is available at most supermarkets.

½ cup currants
½ cup golden raisins
½ cup apricots, cut into small (about ¼-inch) pieces
2 boxes Near East Wheat Pilaf mix
About 6 tablespoons olive oil
1 cup pecans, coarsely chopped
½ cup finely chopped flat-leaf parsley
¼ cup finely sliced green onion
1 tablespoon minced orange zest
About 4 tablespoons orange juice
Coarse or kosher salt and ground black pepper

1. Evenly scatter the dried fruit on a sheet pan and set aside.

2. Cook the pilaf according to package directions. When the pilaf is done, spoon the grain over the fruit (the steam will soften and plump the fruit). Allow the pilaf to cool completely and dry out thoroughly.

3. When the pilaf is dry, transfer it to a large mixing bowl. Add 2 tablespoons of oil and toss, adding a little more oil as necessary, until the wheat granules are separate and coated with oil.

4. In a small, heavy skillet, warm 2 tablespoons of oil over low heat. Add the pecans and cook, stirring occasionally, until the nuts are toasted, about 4 minutes (they should be deeply browned but not burned).

5. Immediately add the hot pecans to the bowl, but do not mix. Sprinkle the parsley, green onion, and orange zest over the pilaf and toss to combine. Add orange juice, salt, and pepper to taste, and toss again.

SERVES 6 TO 8

ASPARAGUS AND PORTOBELLO SALAD

The olive oil and browned shallots clinging to the mushrooms will also season the asparagus, eliminating the need for a vinaigrette or other dressing on this earthy salad. Note that you sauté the shallots and mushrooms in two batches so that they aren't crowded in the pan.

2 lb. medium-thin asparagus (about 45 stalks)
1 lb. portobello mushrooms
2 tablespoons unsalted butter
4 tablespoons olive oil
3 shallots, finely chopped
Coarse or kosher salt and ground black pepper

1. Trim the woody ends from the asparagus and cut the stalks on the diagonal into 1-inch pieces, keeping the tips intact. Trim and clean the mushrooms and cut into large dice. You will have about 4 cups of each.

2. Prepare an ice bath by combining 3 trays of ice cubes and 3 cups (or more) of ice water in a large mixing bowl. In a medium stockpot of lightly salted boiling water, blanch the asparagus until bright green and crisp-tender, about 2 minutes. Immediately drain the asparagus in a colander, then drop it into the ice bath. When the asparagus is cool, drain it and spread it out to dry on sheet pans lined with paper towels. Leave at room temperature until ready to serve.

3. In a large, heavy skillet over medium-high heat melt half the butter with half the oil until foamy. Add half the shallots and cook until fragrant and lightly colored. Add half the mushrooms and cook until golden. Transfer to a mixing bowl and cook the remaining shallots and mushrooms in the remaining butter and oil. Add salt and pepper to taste; set aside at room temperature.

4. About 45 minutes before serving time, combine the asparagus and mushrooms, adding more salt and pepper if needed.

SERVES 6 TO 8

The Outdoor Option

The herbed chicken lends itself to an outdoor meal, but even the most enthusiastic outdoor chef has to accept the fact that there comes a point when standing over a grill becomes more problematic than pleasurable. Depending on the size of your grill and your level of expertise, that probably happens when you're cooking for eight to twelve guests. At larger gatherings, timing a main course can mean devoting all your free time to the grill at the expense of actually entertaining your guests. (Standing around and watching you cook and worry is not as amusing as you may think.) You can take the heat off and still be a grill hero if you make the main course ahead of time—in the kitchen—and save the fancy grill work for appetizers or side dishes (prepped ahead of time and grilled during cocktails for maximum drama with minimum trauma).

Stacking Textures

Platters of simple grilled vegetables make a valuable contribution to any table—they're beautiful and colorful, decorative as well as delicious. Grilled endive and radicchio accented with sweet red onions make a nice change from the ubiquitous grilled eggplant, peppers, and zucchini. Dessert can be as simple as lemon gelato with fresh blackberries.

Outdoor Hors d'Oeuvre

There is a time and a place for elaborately constructed hors d'oeuvre, but a hot summer night in your backyard is neither. Keep it simple. If you want to use the grill, brush sliced country bread with garlic-infused olive oil and grill it over a medium fire until crisp and slightly charred on the edges, 5 to 6 minutes. You don't have to be a culinary genius to know that the smell of grilled bread makes people hungry, so make plenty.

When you can stop passing hot bread right into the greedy hands of those gathering around the grill, pile the rest on a platter and surround it with sweet and salty prosciutto and small chunks of nutty Parmigiano-Reggiano or a sharp provolone. Add savory black and green olives (see page 22), and you've got enough to keep the most ravenous guest busy until it's time to go to the table.

GRILLED ENDIVE, RADICCHIO, AND RED ONION

Unlike beef or lamb kebabs, which need the heat conducted by metal skewers to cook the meat through, vegetables just need to be held in place, so bamboo skewers work fine. Choose small, compact heads of Belgian endive (with pale leaves and yellowish-green tips) and Treviso radicchio (a variety with long, tapered leaves versus radicchio di Verona, which forms round, lettuce-like heads). This is a good opportunity to use an infused olive oil, such as one flavored with rosemary, garlic, or black pepper.

> 4 heads Belgian endive
> 4 small heads Treviso radicchio
> Olive oil
> Kosher or coarse salt and ground black pepper
> 4 medium red onions

1. Trim the stems of the endives. Split the endives and radicchio lengthwise without cutting through the root ends. Toss the endives and radicchio with oil (enough so they're lightly coated but not dripping), salt, and pepper, and set aside for at least 45 minutes before grilling.

2. Peel the onions and cut into ⅓-inch slices. Slide the skewers through the layers, making onion "lollipops." Marinate in oil, salt, and pepper for at least 45 minutes.

3. Grill the endives cut-side up over a medium-hot fire for 3 minutes, then turn and grill for about 3 minutes longer, or until browned (turn them only once). Repeat with the radicchio. Transfer to a serving platter, fanning out the radicchio first and then adding a row of endive. Repeat until you have covered the surface of the plate.

4. Grill the onions over a medium-hot fire until lightly charred, 6 to 8 minutes. Slide the onions off the skewers and onto the serving platter, arranging them over the endive and radicchio.

SERVES 6 TO 8

BASIL-GRILLED CHERRY TOMATOES

In late summer, the shrub-sized bunches of fresh basil at farm markets are just too seductive to resist. Wrapping the leaves around tomatoes might seem a little fussy, but it infuses the tomatoes with herb flavor in a way nothing else can.

1 pint (about 32) ripe cherry tomatoes
1 bunch (at least 32 separate leaves) fresh basil, washed and dried
Olive oil
Salt and ground black pepper

1. Rinse and dry the tomatoes. Wrap each tomato in a basil leaf, overlapping the leaf's tip and stem (it should be snug but not pulled tight). Run a skewer through this overlap, threading three tomato-basil bundles on each skewer.

2. Place the skewered tomatoes in a shallow baking dish and drizzle with oil (rotating the skewers to coat all sides), salt, and pepper. Marinate for at least 45 minutes.

3. Grill over a medium-hot fire until the tomatoes are soft and the basil leaves lose their bright green color, 8 to 10 minutes. Transfer—skewer and all—to a small serving platter.

SERVES 6 TO 8

5/Southwestern Pork Tenderloin
➤ Twice-baked Potatoes
➤ Skillet Slaw

In the late nineties, I took a "writing" test in order to get freelance work for a famous restaurant survey company: "writing" the pithy paragraphs that pass for reviews. Although I have blocked out the machinations of exactly how that worked, I can still see the pages and pages of survey comments from the restaurant-going public that I had to read before I could construct one of those dense little paragraphs. The comments arrived on enormous stacks of paper, and if the responses hadn't been so unintentionally funny, they would have been tragic. Why did anyone think such over-the-top comments and cringe-inducing attempts at humor made for good reviews?

The truth is that the survey respondents were doing nothing more (and yet so much less) than emulating the restaurant reviewers they read and worshipped. Restaurant criticism is not an easy thing to do, but since everyone eats, I suppose the respondents felt inherently qualified to comment. However, the ability to translate taste into words (that people can understand) is a rare skill, and even the pros sound silly every once in a while. While the "writing" job (covering the two-hundred-and-ten restaurants that started with the letter "C") was over in six weeks, the experience (as well as the immersion into such market-driven restaurant criticism) has stayed with me, and I have come to eye any restaurant review—survey, guide, magazine, or newspaper—with well-earned skepticism.

Even so, when I saw a write-up in the paper for a new traditional *taqueria* in my neighborhood (an uptown stretch of New York City's Amsterdam Avenue christened "Little Mexico") that the reviewer claimed was much more "authentic" than the Americanized Mexican places on nearby Broadway, I insisted that my friend Wayne meet me there for lunch. "I'm not sure exactly where it is, somewhere on Amsterdam around 107th Street," I told him. "I'll just find it and wait outside for you." He arrived, and we walked into the dark *taqueria*—the only people there—and sat at a small table with a sticky glass square covering a stained cloth (not a good sign). We sat for a long time waiting for someone, anyone, to appear. Jumping to the worst conclusion, I blamed the reviewer. How like this particular guy, I thought, one of those "food intellectuals" who prides himself on "discovering" ethnic and offbeat places and then patronizing them in every sense of the word, to describe a dump like this as "authentic." Then Wayne leaned across the table and delivered his own succinct review, "Sweetie, it smells like a men's room." We left.

When I got home, I looked up the review again: It wasn't 107th Street; it was 102nd. The next day I went to the right restaurant, which couldn't have been cleaner, friendlier, or more wonderfully "authentic." I have eaten there many times since and am never disappointed. After tasting their pork tenderloin, I am slowly learning to trust reviews (and reviewers) again.

Stacking Textures

When American farmers started breeding leaner pigs, the fat content of pork was lowered by about 30 percent. As a result, most pork, especially the tenderloin, is ultra lean. Although wonderfully seasoned, it can use the rich creaminess bestowed by twice-baked potatoes and the slightly tangy dressing of the warm slaw. For dessert: To set off the spices in the Southwestern rub, try ginger spice cookies (page 163) served with coffee ice cream.

Social Scenario

The beauty of this meal goes beyond taste to its ease of service. It's an ideal menu for occasions when you would like to have a larger sit-down meal (and not be limited to a buffet). The uniformly rolled and tied boneless pork is simpler and quicker to slice than a roast with a bone, the potatoes are individually portioned, and the slaw goes quickly from skillet to plate. You can individually plate this meal in the kitchen (this kind of service is called "American style"), or arrange the food on platters and place them right on the table, allowing guests to help themselves family style.

SOUTHWESTERN PORK TENDERLOIN

A pork tenderloin is an ultra-lean cylinder of meat that usually weighs about 1 pound. Although the tenderloin is, as its name suggests, a tender cut, it is not particularly flavorful and benefits from a spicy dry rub. This particular seasoning blend contains the same spices as chili, adding a Southwestern touch. Rub the mixture into the tenderloin and leave it at room temperature for at least an hour; the spices should be absorbed by the time you cook the pork. You can also rub on the spice blend the day before, then wrap and refrigerate the tenderloin overnight: The longer it sits, the more intense the flavor becomes.

> **2 tablespoons kosher salt**
> **1 tablespoon chili powder**
> **1 tablespoon ground cumin**
> **1 tablespoon granulated garlic**
> **1 tablespoon finely ground black pepper**
> **¾ teaspoon unsweetened cocoa powder (Hershey's is fine)**
> **3 pork tenderloins, about 1 lb. each**
> **About 1 tablespoon olive oil**

1. Combine the salt, chili powder, cumin, garlic, pepper, and cocoa, and rub the mixture on the tenderloins, lightly coating the entire surface. Let stand at room temperature for at least an hour.

2. Preheat the oven to 350°F. Pour just enough oil into a heavy ovenproof skillet to coat the bottom with a thin film of oil. Warm the oil over medium-high heat until hot but not smoking: The oil must be hot enough to brown the meat without burning the spice rub. One at a time, sear the tenderloins on all sides, 3 to 5 minutes. Immediately transfer to a heavy-gauge sheet pan, place in the oven, and roast until the pork is cooked through. Medium-well will take about 18 minutes—an instant-read meat thermometer inserted into the thickest part of the tenderloin will read 160°F.

3. Remove the pan from the oven and let the tenderloins rest for about 10 minutes. Carve into thick slices (medallions).

SERVES 6 TO 8

PORK TACOS

Pork tenderloin is endlessly adaptable and also tastes great with the classic steakhouse rub (page 42) or any of the commercial blends you can buy in fancy food markets or butcher shops. Any Southwestern spice combination will help turn a tenderloin into great pork tacos. Start assembling the tacos while the tenderloin is still warm.

> 1 pork tenderloin, about 1 lb., dry-rubbed and roasted
> 8 (6-inch) corn tortillas
> 1 cup shredded romaine lettuce
> ½ cup finely chopped white onion
> ¼ cup cleaned cilantro leaves, torn into little pieces
> 8 lime wedges

1. While the pork rests after roasting, warm a small skillet over low heat. Using tongs, and working one at a time, warm the tortillas for about 5 seconds on each side (they should be slightly flexible).

2. Place 2 tortillas on each of 2 plates, overlapping them with about 1 inch separating the edges. Evenly divide the romaine, onion, and cilantro, and arrange in a narrow strip along the center of the tortillas.

3. Cut the pork tenderloin into thick (about ⅓-inch) slices and then into strips. Top the tortillas with pork and a squeeze of lime juice.

MAKES 4 PORK TACOS, AND SERVES 2 HEARTY EATERS

SKILLET SLAW

Cremini mushrooms (also called Italian brown mushrooms) are small portobellos about the size of white button mushrooms. Bagged shredded cabbage and carrots are available in the produce department of most large supermarkets. The vegetables are cooked by a method akin to stir-frying, with small amounts of oil added as needed. The vegetables may stick to the pan at first, but add the oil very sparingly or the slaw will be soggy.

4 tablespoons olive oil
¾ lb. cremini mushrooms, wiped clean, trimmed, and thinly sliced (about 1½ cups)
1 large red onion, peeled and finely chopped (about 1 cup)
6 medium carrots, trimmed, peeled, and shredded (about 3 cups)
1 medium head white cabbage, trimmed, cored, and shredded (about 6 cups)
4 tablespoons red wine vinegar
2 tablespoons sugar
Coarse or kosher salt
Ground black pepper
Snipped fresh chives (optional, for garnish)

1. In a large heavy skillet over medium heat, warm 1 tablespoon of oil until hot but not smoking. Add the mushrooms and cook until golden brown, 3 to 5 minutes.

2. Transfer the mushrooms to a large mixing bowl. Return the skillet to the heat and add a bit more oil. Cook the onion, carrots, and cabbage separately by the same method, transferring each vegetable to the mixing bowl when finished.

3. Return the skillet to the heat and quickly deglaze it (see page 47) with vinegar, using a flat sauce whisk or wooden spoon to scrape up any browned bits in the bottom of the pan. Add the sugar and whisk until it dissolves. Pour the sauce over the vegetables and toss to coat. Add salt and pepper to taste and toss again. Garnish with chives, if desired, and serve immediately.

SERVES 6 TO 8

TWICE-BAKED POTATOES

This recipe serves one. For multiple servings, the potatoes should be as uniform as possible to ensure even cooking times (and end arguments about whose is biggest). Use a bright orange Cheddar, which will color the potato as it melts.

> 1 large well-shaped Idaho baking potato, washed, dried, and lightly pierced with a fork
> 2 teaspoons unsalted butter, softened
> 2 tablespoons heavy cream
> 2 tablespoons shredded extra-sharp Cheddar
> 1 tablespoon finely chopped flat-leaf parsley
> Coarse or kosher salt and ground black pepper to taste

1. Preheat the oven to 450°F. Bake the potato until tender, about 45 minutes. Set aside until cool enough to handle.

2. Reduce the oven temperature to 350°F. Using a serrated knife, cut into the potato lengthwise to make an oval opening. Scoop out the flesh, being careful not to tear the skin. Mash the potato with butter and cream until as smooth as you like (some like it lumpy). Fold in the cheese, parsley, and salt and pepper to taste. Re-stuff the potato, place it in a shallow pan, and bake until golden brown and puffy, about 15 minutes.

MAKES 1

Everyday Meals

4

Everyday Meals
Recipes for Any Occasion

Onion Soup

It's no secret that Parisians are willing to rally around their city as a bastion of haute cuisine. But they are also willing to fight to preserve the inherent culture in even the most ordinary food.

When Le Balzar, the old Left Bank brasserie, was bought by Groupe Flo (a large restaurant chain that specializes in buying and then modernizing old brasseries), Les Amis du Balzar, a group of the brasserie's loyal patrons, staged a dinnertime uprising against the new management. To the five hundred members of Le Amis du Balzar, the authentic spirit of a restaurant is not only in the space, but in the food itself, and the committee wanted it known that they would tolerate no change in their social or gastronomic lives, particularly in the guise of "improvements."

If this seems extreme, consider the fate of onion soup (a staple of Parisian café life) in our own country. As a culinary souvenir of America's mid-fifties European travel boom, this classic dish met our mass-produced mainstream culture and became "French onion soup:" a pale, thin liquid barely able to float its rubbery lump of melted cheese and sodden bread.

Once a nobly heroic and honest dish, onion soup was a poor man's meal: a robust broth enhanced by caramelized onions (one of the world's cheapest flavor sources) and topped with a thin crust of toasted bread and melted cheese. In Les Halles, the old market described by the writer Emile Zola as the "belly of Paris," where restaurants were open in the early hours of the morning to feed *"les vicieux"* (the butchers,

fishmongers and porters whose heavy labor kept the market running), onion soup was known for its restorative powers—a *soupe de santé,* salvation not only for working stiffs also but for late-night revelers who believed the soup could ward off a hangover. In the bistros and cafés of Les Halles, no matter whether you had just passed a long night or were facing a long day, onion soup was the remedy.

Stacking Textures

This recipe may help in righting our national onion soup wrongs: The traditional rich broth is enhanced with a few sprigs of fresh tarragon and a small amount of heavy cream (whisked in at the end of the cooking to further thicken the soup and accentuate the sweetness of the caramelized onions). Serve it minus the toast-and-cheese topping as a first course with a sprinkle of grated Parmigiano-Reggiano and garlic toasts on the side, or garnish with finely chopped fresh shallots and pair with toasted black bread and a tangy goat cheese.

Cooking Strategy

Peeling and cutting onions is wet work, but if you want to avoid crying into the soup, try burning a candle near your cutting board or holding a newly extinguished kitchen match between your teeth.

THE EQUIPMENT: ONION SOUP BOWLS
To gratinée, use special onion soup bowls that can withstand the heat of the broiler. Available in most kitchen supply stores, the traditional style is the prettiest—a big-bellied white porcelain bowl atop a graceful pedestal. The knob-like handles on each side are often shaped like lion heads.

ONION SOUP

If you've never liked onion soup, consider it your duty to try this one: Just close your eyes and think of Paris.

> 3 tablespoons unsalted butter
> 3 large red onions, peeled and thinly sliced (3 cups)
> 3 large yellow onions, peeled and thinly sliced (about 3 cups)
> ½ teaspoon kosher salt
> ½ teaspoon freshly ground black pepper
> 2 tablespoons flour
> 8 cups superior beef stock
> 2 sprigs fresh tarragon
> ¼ cup heavy cream, at room temperature

1. In a medium stockpot over medium heat, melt the butter until foamy. Add the onions and cook, stirring occasionally, until tender and lightly colored, about 30 minutes. Season with salt and pepper.

2. Sprinkle the flour over the onions and cook, stirring constantly, until the flour is completely absorbed, about 3 minutes. Add the stock and tarragon, increase the heat, and bring to a boil. Lower the heat and simmer until the broth is infused with onion flavor, about 30 minutes.

3. Remove the pot from the heat; discard the tarragon. Slowly whisk in the cream until smooth. Return the pot to the stove and simmer over low heat until slightly thickened, 8 to 10 minutes. Adjust the seasonings to taste.

SERVES 4 TO 6

. . . GRATINÉE, IF YOU MUST

PER PORTION:
> Sliced crusty French bread (about ½ inch thick), toasted on both sides
> ⅓ cup shredded Swiss cheese, such as Emmental or Gruyère

1. Preheat the broiler.

2. Put individual heatproof crocks on a heavy-gauge sheet pan or in a roasting pan. Ladle a portion of hot soup into each crock, top with toasted bread, and sprinkle with cheese. Slide the pan under the broiler and cook until the cheese is melted and bubbly, about 90 seconds. Keep an eye on the cheese, which can go from golden-brown to scorched in seconds.

Fish Tacos

Even before the recent increased security measures turned flying into a crapshoot of inconvenience, I rarely left New York. And when I did, it was usually to go to Los Angeles.

The moment I step out of the climate-controlled terminal at LAX and into the soft Southern California air, I feel slightly thinner and totally irresponsible. Unlike most of my friends, who make fun of the smog and the traffic, I love L.A.

Perhaps it is because I was indoctrinated into Southern California culture by beach movies: first by Moondoggie and Gidget (James Darren and Sandra Dee in director Paul Wendkos' 1959 film, *Gidget,* which spawned the 1965 television show starring Sally Field as Francine "Gidget" Lawrence), and then the Penn-ultimate stoner-surfer, Jeff Spicoli (Sean Penn directed by Cameron Crowe in the 1982 high school classic, *Fast Times at Ridgemont High*). Maybe I've never had a gnarly ride or been clamshelled by an epic wave, but I confess to more than a few fashion moments involving a puka shell anklet. Although I can only fantasize about what surfing actually feels like, I know exactly how it tastes: like a fish taco from one of the beach-shack stands along the Pacific Coast Highway.

Unlike the tidier soft pork tacos (Page 115), fish tacos are wet and messy, clearly meant to be eaten on a beach while an ocean full of wash water laps at your toes. You flake cooked fish into bite-sized pieces, wrap them in warm corn tortillas with some shredded green cabbage (stays crunchier longer than lettuce), and add a layer of chipotle sour cream sauce. The result is way up there in the "excellent" category and just what I want to be eating while I wait for the perfect wave. So what if I can't hang ten? I can eat two.

FISH TACOS

Chipotles in adobo are smoked jalapeño peppers packed in a tomato-based Mexican sauce with a rich, smoky flavor. Chipotles are hot, so adjust the quantity to your taste. You'll find corn tortillas in the refrigerator case of most large supermarkets and at Mexican food stores. If you opt for the onion garnish, don't substitute yellow or other sharp-tasting onions for white ones; the flavor you're looking for is mild, almost sweet.

4 canned chipotles in adobo, plus 2 tablespoons of the adobo sauce
½ cup sour cream
8 (6-inch) corn tortillas
1 cup thinly shredded green cabbage
¼ cup washed cilantro leaves, torn into little pieces
1¼ lb. cooked fish, pulled apart in large flakes
½ cup finely chopped fresh tomatoes and ½ cup finely chopped white onion
  (optional, for garnish)

1. Combine the chipotles, adobo sauce, and sour cream in the bowl of a small food processor fitted with a metal blade; process until smooth.

2. Warm a small skillet over low heat. Using tongs, and working one at a time, warm the tortillas for about 5 seconds on each side (they should be slightly flexible).

3. Place two tortillas on each of two plates, overlapping them with about 1 inch separating the edges. Evenly divide the cabbage and cilantro, and arrange in a narrow strip along the center of the tortillas. Top the tortillas with fish, tomatoes and onions to taste, and a dollop of chipotle sour cream.

MAKES 4 FISH TACOS AND SERVES 2 HEARTY EATERS

PEPPERED PEACHES

Adapted from a Lee Bailey recipe, this West Indian dish is an unusual but well-suited side for the fish tacos or just about anything grilled—poultry, meat, pork, fish. Although the peaches don't keep well, they are easy to make at the last minute. You can adjust the peppery heat to suit your taste; start with the suggested amounts of black pepper and cayenne and then add more, if you like.

> **6 large peaches, relatively ripe but not soft (should be firm but yield to gentle pressure)**
> **3 tablespoons fresh lemon juice**
> **2 tablespoons sugar combined with 1 teaspoon kosher salt**
> **½ teaspoon coarsely ground black pepper, or more to taste**
> **¼ teaspoon cayenne pepper, or more to taste**

1. To peel the peaches: Bring a small stockpot of water to a rolling boil. Meanwhile, cut each peach in half around the seam (stopping at the pit). Holding the peach in both hands, twist slightly to separate the halves. Remove the pit (if you're lucky, it will pop out). Using a slotted spoon, dip each peach half into the boiling water for about 2 seconds. The skins should slip off easily; if they don't, peel them off with a sharp paring knife. Drain the peaches in a colander, then place them cut-side down on paper towels to dry.

2. Place the peach halves cut-side up on a large platter. Coat the cut surface with lemon juice and dust with the sugar mixture. Sprinkle lightly with the black pepper and cayenne. The peaches can be left at room temperature for 2 hours before serving. Do not refrigerate.

MAKES 12

Meatloaf

As if the American-retro food fad isn't annoying enough, newspaper style sections periodically feel compelled to waste gallons of ink exploring the meatloaf as metaphor when all it really takes is a one-sentence explanation from a politician on the campaign trail.

While campaigning in the Midwest prior to the 1999 Straw Poll, Republican presidential hopeful Gary Bauer, asked to share his strategy, replied, "Eating meatloaf all over Iowa, I guess," succinctly delivering the message that meatloaf symbolizes mainstream America. Meatloaf is Everyman's dish, and as such, it's only right that every man ought to know how to make it.

Like that other great Everyman dish, chili, meatloaf suffers from "secret ingredient syndrome," and amateur as well as professional cooks claim you'll never guess what makes their meatloaf stand out. "Crushed pineapple," one guy told me after I was forced to take a bite of his masterpiece and found myself too choked up to speak.

But making the best meatloaf doesn't mean making the most bizarre meatloaf. It means buying quality ingredients and doing as little as possible to them. For beef, choose ground round, with just enough fat content to give you the right texture and consistency; the pork must be fresh enough to still be full of natural juices. Mixing the ingredients thoroughly and then shaping the mixture with a firm touch will give you a compact meatloaf that doesn't crumble when sliced.

Although some may prefer a free-form meatloaf baked in a shallow pan, I take the "loaf" part seriously, using a 9 x 5 x 3-inch metal bread pan. You can buy two-part meatloaf pans; the smaller insert pan is perforated to let juices drain off into the larger pan. However, I use a regular loaf pan, preferring to allow the meatloaf to sit after baking and reabsorb some of those juices.

Good meatloaf is a straightforward dish with flavors that vary from region to region and family to family. People take their meatloaf personally, and for many, it represents the archetypal childhood meal: soothing to eat and soothing to make, a reminder of earlier and easier days. Randy Garbin, publisher of *By the Way,* a journal devoted to preserving the American diner and other such endangered species, sums up his formula for returning to the simple life as follows: "Eat in diners; ride trains; shop on Main Street; put a porch on your house; and live in a walkable community." Maybe he should add, "and make meatloaf."

MEATLOAF

Always let meatloaf sit for 15 to 20 minutes before serving, so that it can reabsorb some of the juices. Then drain away the excess by holding the top of the meatloaf with a kitchen towel and tipping the pan.

2 lb. ground beef (round)
1 lb. ground pork (shoulder)
1 cup dry unseasoned breadcrumbs
1 tablespoon unsalted butter
1 tablespoon olive oil
1½ cups finely chopped yellow onion (3 medium onions)
2 cloves garlic, finely chopped
3 tablespoons Worcestershire sauce
3 tablespoons tomato paste
½ cup finely chopped flat-leaf parsley
2 teaspoons coarse or kosher salt
2 teaspoons ground black pepper
2 large eggs, lightly beaten

1. Preheat the oven to 350°F and lightly spray a 9 x 5 x 3-inch loaf pan with nonstick cooking spray, wiping out the excess with a paper towel.

2. Place the meat in a large bowl and sprinkle with the bread crumbs; set aside. In a medium sauté pan over medium heat, melt the butter with the oil until foamy. Add the onions and garlic and cook until fragrant and lightly colored, about 5 minutes. Add the onion mixture to the meat but do not combine.

3. In a small mixing bowl, combine the Worcestershire sauce, tomato paste, parsley, salt, pepper, and eggs, and beat lightly. Pour this mixture over the meat and onions and mix it thoroughly with your hands. Press the mixture gently into the pan, making sure it fills the corners. Bake until the meatloaf has a brown top crust and is cooked through, 60 to 70 minutes (an instant-read meat thermometer inserted into the thickest part of the meatloaf should read 160°F).

SERVES 4 TO 6

Meatballs

The first time I met Jim's new girlfriend, I knew he would end up marrying her. Although Jim and I had been friends for fifteen years, it wasn't anything in *his* behavior that made me realize that their wedding was a done deal. It was what I saw in *her*. Joanne was an Italian-American neighborhood girl from an outer borough of New York City who had managed to crack the inner circle of Hollywood; she was a self-starting, go-getting talent agent by day, and an old-fashioned, soft-hearted girlfriend by night.

Apparently Joanne could do it all. Except cook. Well, it wasn't that she couldn't cook. It's just that she would rather make a deal than dinner, and so whenever I went to Los Angeles, it was my pleasure to cook for her. She may have been a born businesswoman and a scary negotiator, but I didn't find Joanne hard to please. At the bottom of it all, she and I shared the same red-sauce sensibility: We both loved meatballs.

I was in Los Angeles the night Jim proposed, and early the next morning Joanne got right down to the business of being a bride. From under her bed she pulled the pile of bridal magazines she had been buying since the day she met Jim, and we pored over the pictures. I even went shopping with her, and we smiled at each other while the cashmere-clad saleswoman chattered on about chantilly-lace bodices with subtle ruching at the waist and ivory duchesse satin columns. Although neither of us had any idea what that saleswoman meant, when we sat down to dinner that night and went over dress details, I made sure we were on familiar ground. Although a big dish like spaghetti and meatballs seemed out of place in sushi-intensive, Zone-dieting Los Angeles, Joanne and I made no apologies about enjoying our home-town favorite. We may have been two girls adrift in a sea of silk gazar, but when it came to food we knew what was what. And it didn't have to be gussied up to look good to us.

USE EVERYTHING

FOR BUFFETS: Make the meatballs smaller, about the diameter of a quarter, and cook them for about 8 minutes. You'll get about 40 meatballs that are easier to eat while standing.

FOR THE FUTURE: Once you turn out a batch of these meatballs, you can use what you need and freeze the rest in an airtight plastic bag. To reheat: Defrost the number of meatballs you want to use, and preheat the oven to 325°F. Place the meatballs in a shallow baking dish (large enough so they have room to roll around). Bake until warmed through, about 6 minutes, shaking the dish occasionally to expose all sides of the meatballs. Drop the warmed meatballs into your sauce.

MOST EXCELLENT MEATBALLS

For spaghetti and meatballs: To serve six adults, you'll need about one pound of dried pasta and about six cups of your favorite sauce, from a jar or homemade. Cook the pasta in a big pot of abundantly salted water according to the package directions (it should be al dente); drain but do not rinse. Return the pasta to the pot and toss with half the sauce until well coated. Transfer the spaghetti to warmed plates and top with the remaining sauce, dividing the meatballs evenly—or not.

1 lb. ground beef
1 lb. sweet Italian pork sausage, removed from casing
1 cup seasoned dry breadcrumbs
2 eggs, lightly beaten
⅓ cup grated Parmigiano-Reggiano
¼ cup finely chopped flat-leaf parsley
1 teaspoon coarse or kosher salt
1 teaspoon ground black pepper

1. Preheat the broiler. In a large bowl, combine the beef and sausage, mixing well. Sprinkle the breadcrumbs over the meat and blend in carefully. Pour the eggs over the mixture, then add the grated cheese, parsley, salt, and pepper, and mix until well combined.

2. Shape the mixture into balls—large than golf, smaller than tennis. Use your flattened palms to gently roll each meatball until it is "seamless." Put the meatballs in a shallow metal pie tin (make sure they have room to roll around); a standard 9-inch tin will hold about 6 at a time.

3. Broil the meatballs for 12 to 15 minutes, occasionally shaking the pan gently to expose all sides of the meatballs to the broiler. (Even carnivores like me need to put aside our make-it-rare preferences; meatballs are always well-done.) Drain the cooked meatballs on paper towels. Reheat in hot tomato sauce (a/k/a "gravy" in Italian-American households) before serving.

MAKES ABOUT 18 MEATBALLS

Chicken Enchilada Casserole

I once got a call from a friend asking if I would be interested in helping test some recipes for lifestyle guru Lee Bailey to use in his new cookbook. Was he kidding? Hadn't I been a high-falutin' caterer for over a decade? Wasn't I sure I had a million ideas that were oh-so-right for Lee Bailey? And when I sat down across the table from Mr. Bailey, spouting all those ideas, there was no doubt about how perfect they were for him—they were his.

Long before lifestyles could be purchased, before catalog collections were contrived in order to provide your home with a complete "look," people had to rely on taste, and, like so many other New Yorkers, I relied on Lee Bailey's. The Lee Bailey Shop (which he referred to as a "glamorous hardware store") in Henri Bendel (the fabulous old 57th Street location) was filled with his signature look in housewares: clean, classic American design.

In 1983, Lee Bailey applied his sensibility to food, flowers and other fundamentals of good living by publishing his landmark entertaining book, *Lee Bailey's Country Weekends.* By the time he retired there were fifteen more Bailey books, each devoted to unpretentious and beautifully photographed food, and I was lucky enough to work on several of them. On the days we prepared the food for photography, we did not squirt truffle oil in the shape of Wyoming under the meatloaf; we did not twist the vegetables into origami; we did not paint grill marks on the scallops. In fact, we did nothing more dramatic than transfer the food from the oven to the particular plate Mr. Bailey had chosen. A cake could be lopsided, a pie might come out with a less-than-perfect crust, but it was still considered ready for its close-up.

Cooking Strategy

Lee Bailey's natural attitude toward food, even food destined to feed a party crowd, is the inspiration behind this chicken enchilada casserole, my interpretation of one of his recipes. I think of it as Southwestern lasagna because it's all there: the layers (made with tortillas instead of noodles), the melted cheese (Jack and Cheddar instead of ricotta and Parmesan), the tomato sauce (only with the tang of chilies and brown sugar, like a Mexican *mole* sauce). The dish also has all the best party properties of lasagna: It can be made the day before and served plated or from a buffet. If you plan on serving this dish at a buffet, invest in a rectangular ceramic baking dish, which looks so much better than a metal lasagna pan. Even Mr. Bailey did: It's the only kind of kitchen vanity he would allow.

THE EQUIPMENT: CERAMIC BAKING DISHES
Unlike metal baking pans, which have straight sides, rectangular ceramic baking dishes have sloping sides and rounded edges so you can easily slip a spatula in and under the food for serving. Since they conduct, retain, and diffuse heat well, ceramic dishes can go from refrigerator to oven to table. Ceramic baking dishes usually come with a white interior and "decorator" color exterior, such as French blue or forest green.

CHICKEN ENCHILADA CASSEROLE

Shredding the chicken into bite-size pieces by hand (instead of cutting it with a knife) results in uneven surfaces with better "cling" for sauces and dressings. Buy whole green chilies for the sauce, not the pre-chopped chilies, which don't retain enough oil. You'll notice that you don't stir the onions while they're browning—that's so they caramelize (the sugars on their surface turn brown) to add flavor and texture.

THE SAUCE
1 (28-oz.) can tomato purée
2 tablespoons olive oil
2½ cups diced yellow onion
2 cloves garlic, peeled and minced
2 tablespoons chopped mild (canned) green chilies
2 tablespoons mild chili powder
1 tablespoon dark brown sugar
2 teaspoons coarse or kosher salt
2 teaspoons ground black pepper
½ cup superior chicken stock

THE FILLING
1½ cups shredded Monterey Jack cheese
1½ cups shredded Cheddar cheese
6 cups bite-size pieces of cooked chicken
1½ cups diced red onion
1 teaspoon coarse or kosher salt
1 teaspoon ground black pepper

TO ASSEMBLE
12 (8-inch) flour tortillas

GARNISH
Sour cream and chopped green onions or salsa fresca (well drained)

1. For the sauce, place the tomato purée in a large mixing bowl; set aside. Heat the oil in a large, heavy sauté pan over medium-high heat. When the oil is hot but not smoking, add the yellow onions in a single layer (do not over-crowd; you may have to cook them in two batches) and cook without stirring or turning them until they begin to brown, 5 to 8 minutes.

2. Using a spatula, flip the onions over to brown on the other side, 3 to 5 minutes. The onions should be well colored but not burned. (If you cooked them in two batches, combine them in the sauté pan before continuing.) Lower the heat to medium, add the garlic and chilies to the pan, and continue to cook, stirring frequently, until the garlic begins to color, about 3 minutes. Sprinkle in the chili powder and brown sugar, and cook, stirring constantly, until the mixture takes on a deep, rich color and the onions are well coated, 3 to 5 minutes. Stir in the salt and pepper, then scrape the onion mixture into the bowl of tomato purée and stir to combine.

3. Immediately return the pan to the heat and deglaze the pan with the stock (see page 47), allowing the liquid to come to a boil and stirring with a wooden spoon to scrape up any browned bits. Simmer for several minutes to thicken the stock slightly, then add it to the tomato mixture. Wipe out the pan with paper towels and set aside.

4. In a food processor fitted with a metal blade, working in small batches, process the tomato mixture to make a smooth sauce. Transfer the sauce to a small stockpot (or large saucepan) and bring to a simmer over low heat. (This mixture is very thick and should be stirred constantly while heating. Beware: it will splatter.) Simmer uncovered, stirring frequently and adjusting the heat so the sauce does not burn, until the sauce is thoroughly cooked and the flavors are blended, 15 to 20 minutes. You will have about 4 cups.

5. For the filling, combine the Monterey Jack and Cheddar. Place the chicken in a large mixing bowl and set aside. In the sauté pan, cook the red onions the same way you cooked the yellow ones. Add the red onions to the chicken. When the mixture is completely cooled, add 1½ cups of the cheese and the salt and pepper, and toss to combine.

6. Preheat the oven to 375°F. Lightly brush the sides of a 13 x 10-inch baking dish with oil and spread a thin layer of sauce (about ½ cup) in the bottom.

7. In a small skillet over low heat, working one at a time, soften the tortillas by warming each side for about 30 seconds. Place each tortilla on a clean work surface, spoon 1 tablespoon of sauce along the center, and add about ½ cup of the filling. Roll the tortilla and place it seam-side down in the baking dish. Continue the process until each tortilla is rolled, filled, and securely placed in a single layer. Spread the remaining sauce on top, sprinkle with the remaining cheese, and bake for 35 minutes, or until the top is browned and bubbling. Garnish each portion with sour cream, green onions, and/or salsa, if desired.

SERVES 6

135

Chicken Pot Pie

Picture mid-eighties Manhattan: Cotton was high and cuisine was tall, when suddenly, chicken pot pie began to appear on Limoges dinner plates at the most uptown of parties.

I'm not exactly sure which caterer and hostess teamed up to start this trend, or even why they did. Maybe serving such informal fare in such ritzy settings was meant to be an antidote for too much civilization. But there was something perversely precious about watching the bejeweled and black-tied sit down to a simple dish like chicken pot pie—like reading a glossy magazine spread about rich women who garden. As you can imagine, during those days of excess, nothing stayed simple for long, and as the chicken pot pie trend spread through the Upper East Side, caterers began to compete with each other by tarting up the pie, replacing the regular crust with puff pastry and decorating the top with doughy doodads and curlicues.

It took me almost a decade to stop thinking of chicken pot pie as society's latest dish, and it happened quite by accident. One January night, when New Yorkers were anticipating the season's biggest snowfall, a sick friend asked me to make him some chicken soup. I went to the store, got caught up in the frenzy of pre-storm food shopping and bought much more than I needed. What else could I do? With just a little dough and practically the same ingredients needed for my sick friend's soup, I made chicken pot pie.

As I folded this dish back into my cooking repertoire, I remembered everything I loved about it—the wholesome combination of chicken and vegetables, the smell of a warm, savory pie; and everything I didn't—picking the chicken meat off the bones and making the dough.

Cooking Strategy

Our version relies on ready-made, pre-rolled pie crust (sold in flat disks, not in pie pans, and available in the supermarket refrigerator case) and precooked chicken (whether you cook it yourself or buy it from the supermarket rotisserie). Now, this is not a sin; it's not even a crime. These shortcuts just make it possible for you to turn out an old-fashioned recipe in new-fangled time. If you absolutely feel you must make your own pie crust (or roast your own bird), go ahead, but I'm warning you—you're making this much more difficult than it needs to be.

CHICKEN POT PIE

I'm not kidding about letting these rest 15 to 20 minutes before serving. People usually dig in too soon and end up burning their tongues. So be careful and let the pies cool—the middle of a pot pie is always hotter than you think. Plan ahead: You'll need four 5-inch mini-pie pans for this recipe.

> 2 (9-inch) pie crusts
> About 5 tablespoons flour
> 2½ cups superior chicken stock
> 1 cup diced red potatoes (about 4 small potatoes), scrubbed but not peeled
> 1 cup diced carrot (about 2 medium carrots)
> ½ cup frozen peas (get the tiny, extra fancy; no sauce), thawed and drained
> 2 cups bite-size pieces of cooked chicken
> 2 teaspoons coarse or kosher salt
> 2 teaspoons ground black pepper
> 2 tablespoons unsalted butter
> ½ cup diced onion
> ¼ teaspoon dried thyme
> 1 egg, lightly beaten

1. Place a heavy-gauge sheet pan in the oven and preheat to 375°F. If you are using boxed pie crusts, bring them to room temperature according to the package directions.

2. Place one round of pie-crust dough on a dry, lightly floured surface (use about 2 tablespoons of flour for this) and cut into four sections. Roll each section into a rough circle about 6 inches across (big enough to line a 5-inch pie tin and leave a ½-inch overhang). Line four 5-inch pie tins with the dough.

3. Using the second pie crust, cut and roll 4 top crusts, each about 6 inches across; set aside.

4. In a medium saucepan over medium heat, bring the chicken stock to a boil. Reduce the heat but keep the stock hot.

5. For the filling, in a large saucepan of lightly salted boiling water, cook the potatoes until crisp-tender, about 8 minutes. Using a slotted spoon, remove the potatoes, drain and place in a large mixing bowl. Add the carrots to the still-boiling water and cook until crisp-tender, about 6 minutes, then drain and add to the potatoes. Add the peas, chicken, salt, and pepper to the filling mixture and toss gently to combine.

6. In a small heavy skillet over medium heat, melt the butter until foamy. Add the onions and sauté until they begin to wilt and color slightly on the edges, 5 to 8 minutes. Sprinkle 3 tablespoons of the remaining flour over the onions and cook, stirring constantly, until the flour looks slightly toasted but has not burned, 3 to 5 minutes.

7. Whisk the hot stock (a little at a time) into the flour mixture until smooth. Cook, whisking constantly, until the sauce begins to thicken, about 5 minutes. Remove from the heat and stir in the thyme.

8. Spoon the filling into the pie crusts and pour the sauce over it. Lay the top crusts over the filling and crimp the edges of the dough together, sealing the pies. Trim any ragged edges. Using the tip of a small sharp knife, cut several steam vents (about 2 inches long) in the center of each top crust and brush the crust with beaten egg. Place the pie tins on the hot sheet pan and bake until the crust is a deep golden brown, 25 to 30 minutes. Remove the pan from the oven and cool the pot pies on a rack for at least 15 to 20 minutes before serving.

SERVES 4

Leftover Steak

To a confirmed carnivore like me, proud to fly the fat-stippled flag of red meat at almost every meal, it is hard to imagine such as thing as leftover steak. But if you are lucky enough to possess such a delicious rarity, I believe that you should eat it in the middle of the night by the light of the refrigerator, with a bottle of beer in your hand and a smile on your face.

However, let's say you are one of those organized weekend hosts who have not only cooked an extra steak, but also managed to keep it away from guests like me. If that's anywhere near the truth, you now have the foundation for some great no-work lunches.

Meat "tightens up" when refrigerated, making it easier to slice the steak while it is still cold; but let the sliced beef come to room temperature before you make a sandwich, because it will taste better that way. A few steak sandwich suggestions:

1. Sliced steak topped with Skillet Slaw (page 116) and Chipotle Sour Cream (page 125) on toasted sourdough bread

2. Sliced steak topped with bacon, grilled red onions, romaine lettuce, and Slow-Roasted Tomatoes (page 29) on toasted country white bread with spreadable blue cheese (a French Bleu de Bresse such as Pipo 'Crem, or a Danish Saga Blue)

3. Sliced steak layered with shards of Asiago or Parmigiano-Reggiano, arugula, and roasted peppers on a baguette

4. Sliced steak on garlic bread spread with Green Olive and Walnut Tapenade (page 26)

5. Sliced steak and a layer of barbecued potato chips smashed in a warm onion roll.

THE BEST SANDWICHES

People who need a recipe to get this job done are in deep culinary trouble; making a sandwich is one of the most primal kitchen experiences you can have. But to do true justice to the subject, we must first divide sandwiches into two categories: the purchased (or public) sandwich, and the at-home (or private) sandwich. No matter how uncomplicated and spontaneous the latter may seem, making a private sandwich entails great specificity. "Creamy Skippy peanut butter spread thick on Arnold Country White bread," my friend Justin told me. "I usually eat two of these sandwiches in a sitting and never cut the sandwiches in half. There is no jam or jelly, no bananas, no bacon. The bread is never toasted; it has to be soft, so it can't be old, and it can't have been kept in the refrigerator. This meal is good for anxiety attacks, stomachaches, and sudden hunger brought on by nerves. Also excellent for hangovers."

Great Public Sandwiches

➤ Warm roast pork (dunked in natural juices) and sharp provolone at Di Nic's in Philadelphia's Reading Terminal Market

➤ Number 97: Lisa C's Boisterous Brisket—hand-pulled brisket in barbecue sauce on a challah bun at Zingerman's Deli in Ann Arbor, Michigan

➤ Hot Meatloaf Sandwich from The Kitchen Door in Austin, Texas

➤ Muffuletta—layers of classic Italian cold cuts and olive salad, cut into wedges from a large round crusty loaf of bread—at Central Grocery in New Orleans

➤ The Cubano (pork, ham, and cheese on a roll, melted together in a sandwich press) at Latin American Cafeteria in Miami, Florida

Great Movie Sandwich Moments

➤ When Diane Keaton (as Annie Hall in the 1977 film of the same name) orders a pastrami on white with mayo and lettuce at a Jewish deli, Woody Allen looks embarrassed and then a little afraid.

➤ In the 1984 film, *The Pope of Greenwich Village,* Paulie (Eric Roberts) piles prosciutto and provolone into a split loaf of Italian bread until Charlie (Mickey Rourke) tells him, "You ought to get a permit to shit in the street because you eat like a horse."

➤ The metaphysical musings of Vincent (John Travolta) and Jules (Samuel L. Jackson) on the subject of the cheeseburger royale in Quentin Tarantino's 1994 film, *Pulp Fiction.*

➤ Jack Nicholson (as Robert Dupea) in the 1970 classic *Five Easy Pieces:* A waitress refuses to bring him an off-menu order of toast, so he asks for a chicken salad sandwich on toast and tells the waitress to hold the chicken. "You want me to hold the chicken?" she repeats. "I want you to hold it between your knees."

➤ In the more recent (2000) and almost unbearably heavy-handed film, *The Contender,* the President of the United States (Jeff Bridges) tries to convince an idealistic young congressman (Christian Slater) to share his shark sandwich. (Shark: get it?)

Steak Salad

There aren't many recipe-like rules in the making of a superior steak salad: it is a dish made for improvisation. Over the years, I have developed my own all-purpose framework, using the tiniest roasted new potatoes for heft, just enough diced sweet pepper and green onions to provide brightness, and some chopped celery leaves for their light crispness.

Use medium-rare beef if possible (well-done beef won't absorb dressing), cut into small cubes or strips. Bear in mind that the steak is the star and vegetables just background players. If you used a dry rub or marinade when you cooked the steak, let those specific flavors—be they Pan-Asian or Mediterranean—inspire your choice of vegetables. Cut additions into relatively small pieces so they provide dots of color and texture throughout the salad without becoming the main ingredient.

A good steak salad requires just enough dressing to moisten the meat and provide a flavor thread; there should never be any dressing sitting on the bottom of the plate when you are through. I typically use a classic red-wine vinaigrette (one part red-wine vinegar to three parts olive oil with a touch of grainy mustard and maybe, if I'm feeling industrious, a chopped shallot), although I have used other thin, smooth dressings like herbed buttermilk or creamy garlic with good results. (Thousand Island and Roquefort freaks need not apply; if you are a blue cheese lover, crumble some on top.) If you ever need to stretch your steak salad for unexpected guests, resist the temptation to add mixed greens. Instead, fill out the plates with crisp slices of grilled bread. Trust a beef lover: It is always disappointing when steak salad is made up mostly of salad.

Two Risottos

Once you master the technique for making risotto (see page 52), experimenting with different flavors and add-in ingredients becomes second nature. Keep your risotto light if you intend on serving it as a first course; you can always pair it with grilled or roasted meat as a main. To do it justice, always serve risotto on warmed plates.

ASPARAGUS AND BACON RISOTTO

Although asparagus is now available year round, its delicate but earthy taste was once a culinary harbinger of spring. Pick medium-thin stalks with firm, tightly closed tips, unblemished skin, and moist ends. Along with leeks and onions, asparagus is a member of the lily family; like flowers, asparagus stalks should be kept standing in about an inch of cool water. Store asparagus in the refrigerator and use it within a day or two.

> 4 cups superior chicken stock mixed with 3 cups water
> 4 ounces thick-cut bacon, coarsely chopped
> 4 tablespoons unsalted butter
> 3 shallots, finely chopped
> 2 garlic cloves, finely chopped
> ¾ lb. medium-thin asparagus (about 14 stems), trimmed and cut on the diagonal into 1-inch pieces (tips intact)
> 1½ cups arborio rice
> 1 cup hand-grated Parmigiano-Reggiano
> Coarse or kosher salt and ground black pepper to taste

1. In a heavy saucepan, bring the stock and water to a boil over high heat. Lower the heat under the saucepan, but keep the mixture hot.

2. In a sturdy medium stockpot (at least 8 quarts) over medium heat, cook the bacon until it renders its fat and is almost crisp, 3 to 5 minutes. Remove the bacon and reserve. Drain all but 1 tablespoon of the fat from the pot and add 2 tablespoons of the butter, stirring to combine the fats as the butter melts. When the butter is foamy, add the shallots and garlic and cook, stirring frequently, until golden.

3. In a colander, rinse the asparagus under cool running water. Do not drain. Add the damp asparagus to the stockpot and give the pot a good shake to coat the asparagus with fat. Cover the pot tightly and cook, shaking the pot once or twice, until the asparagus is lightly colored but still crisp-tender, about 3 minutes. Transfer the asparagus, garlic, and shallots to a bowl and set aside.

4. Quickly add the remaining 2 tablespoons of butter to the pot and melt until foamy (adjust the heat so the butter does not burn). Add the rice and stir well to coat.

5. Add 1 cup of hot stock and cook, stirring constantly and scraping up any browned bits from the bottom of the pot, until the liquid is absorbed, 10 to 12 minutes. Continue to cook the rice, adding hot stock ½ cup at a time and stirring until the liquid is absorbed. Quickly stir the asparagus into the rice before adding the last ½ cup of stock. The cooking process will take 30 to 40 minutes; the rice should be tender but still slightly firm to the bite.

6. Remove the risotto from the heat and stir in ½ cup of the grated cheese. Season with salt and pepper. Spoon some risotto into the center of each plate and sprinkle each portion with crumbled bacon and about 1 tablespoon of the grated cheese. Serve immediately, passing extra cheese on the side.

SERVES 2 AS A MAIN COURSE, 4 AS A FIRST

WILD MUSHROOM RISOTTO

The reconstituted dried wild mushrooms and their infused soaking liquid give the risotto an earthy flavor and musky aroma. You can use dried porcini or a blend of dried wild mushrooms. I often buy a variety package called "Wild Forest Mix" that contains shiitake, black trumpets, chanterelles, morels, and porcini. Dried wild mushrooms are typically sold in clear plastic bags. Turn the bag upside down and take a close look to make sure most of the mushrooms are whole or in big pieces rather than crumbs and fragments.

> 2 ounces dried wild mushrooms
> 4 cups superior beef stock
> 2 cups water
> 2 tablespoons butter
> 2 shallots, peeled and minced
> 1½ cups arborio rice
> ½ cup dry white wine
> 1 cup hand-grated Parmigiano-Reggiano
> Coarse or kosher salt and ground black pepper to taste
> 2 tablespoons chopped flat-leaf parsley

1. Place the mushrooms in a small heatproof bowl and cover with 2 cups of boiling water. Let stand until the mushrooms have softened, at least 45 minutes. Remove the mushrooms, gently squeezing out excess liquid, and transfer to a small bowl. Strain the soaking liquid into a bowl through a double thickness of cheesecloth or a paper coffee filter; set aside.

2. Rinse the mushrooms free of any embedded dirt, then drain and chop (you can do this in a small food processor fitted with a metal blade as long as you don't pulverize them). In a heavy saucepan, combine the stock, water, and 1 cup of the mushroom-soaking liquid, and bring to a boil over high heat. Lower the heat, but keep the mixture hot.

3. In a medium stockpot over medium heat, melt the butter until foamy. Add the shallots and cook until soft and lightly colored, 3 to 5 minutes. Stir in the mushrooms and cook until warmed (but not browned) and coated with butter, about 3 minutes. Add the rice and stir to coat with butter. Add the wine and cook, stirring frequently, until the liquid bubbles away.

4. Add 1 cup of the hot stock and cook, stirring, until absorbed, 10 to 12 minutes. Continue to cook the rice, adding hot stock ½ cup at a time and stirring until it is absorbed. The cooking process will take 30 to 40 minutes; the rice should be tender but still slightly firm to the bite.

5. Remove the pot from the heat and stir in ½ cup of the grated cheese. Season with salt and pepper. Spoon risotto into the center of each plate and sprinkle each portion with parsley and about 1 tablespoon of the grated cheese. Serve immediately, passing extra cheese on the side.

SERVES 2 AS A MAIN COURSE, 4 AS A FIRST

Desserts

5

Desserts
Short and Sweet

If you'll bear with me, I think I can explain the role that dessert plays in home entertaining by telling you about the time I went to the terrible wedding of two very nice people.

Even though they are worldly (he went to the Ivy-est League school and speaks French; she sits front-row at fashion shows and speaks Italian), like most couples planning a wedding, they took leave of their senses (most notably, taste) and put themselves in the hands of something called a wedding planner (with a file of "wedding packages").

Fast-forward to the reception. I arrive, accompanied by my good friend, the very social and massively stylish Wayne (wearing, as he pointed out when he picked me up, Prada, Prada, Prada with a scootch of Gucci). We are seated at a table on which a prearranged fruit plate marks each place setting: Not something like delicate slices of melon sprinkled with cracked black pepper and drizzled with a little chestnut honey; this is a hunk of pineapple and a bunch of berries in an arrangement you might see on a Carnival cruise ship. When the waiter removes my plate (untouched), he replaces it with a green salad. Okay. It's odd to follow fruit with salad, but I like this couple, so why not? The salad departs, and in its place we are each presented with a big rimmed soup plate bearing sorbet pressed into the shape of a miniature fruit, speared by a sprig of mint. "Sweetie," Wayne whispers, "What *is* this?" "Sorbet," I shoot back. "But sweetie," he says, raising his eyebrows, "I haven't had anything to eat yet." Lesson: Like sorbet

(classically used as a palate refresher), dessert is not merely decorative; dessert is designed to do something.

Similar to starters, offered in anticipation of what is to come, a dessert should close out the meal, complementing it in both flavor and feeling, leaving your guests feeling sated and yet comfortable. Unless you've done something very wrong, by the time dessert rolls around, your guests have had enough to eat, so there's no need to overwhelm them. Forget the hype—anything described as "deadly," "sinful," "killer," or "to die for." Dessert isn't supposed to hurt you. And forget the height: Keep it short and sweet.

Keeping dessert simple also means making it portable. If guests are able to pick up their plates and move to the couch when the mood strikes, any evening will feel much more comfortable and casual (no matter how serious your intentions). The best desserts for buffet-style entertaining don't even require plates; serving bite-sized sweets will keep guests circulating.

1/Poached Oranges

It might be fruit, but it's not boring. After soaking in the poaching liquid, the oranges take on a silky texture that's pleasing whether they're served chilled, warm, or at room temperature, spooned over ice cream or on their own. The spice-infused citrus syrup adds another dimension to the dessert.

Serving Options
➤ Alone: the oranges, floating in a puddle of syrup, served in a footed glass compote, oversized wine glass, brandy snifter, or shallow bowl
➤ Assisted: as above, with chocolate truffles
➤ On toasted pound cake or warm gingerbread
➤ Over ice cream (quality is everything; pay for super-premium brands), the warm sauce causing the ice cream to melt and get even

creamier. Because there is a spice-infused syrup, think "warm," sophisticated flavors (like pumpkin, ginger, coffee, cinnamon), or something flat-out fancy (like double-deep chocolate peanut butter or *crème brûlée*).

➤ With biscotti or cookies on the side (like the Peanut Butter and Chocolate Kiss Cookies, page 162, or the Ginger Spice Cookies, page 163).

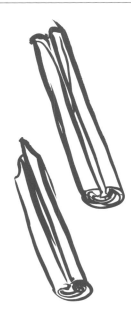

POACHED ORANGES

After you peel the oranges, some web-like white pith will probably remain on the surface. To get rid of it, use a slotted spoon (or a small mesh strainer) to lower the oranges into boiling water for about 5 seconds. Drain in a colander under cold running water and, when cool enough to handle, use a paring knife to scrape off the pith (it will come off easily). Leave the oranges whole, or cut them horizontally into thick slices before proceeding, depending on how you plan to serve them.

8 navel oranges, peel and pith removed
3 cups water
1 ½ cups sugar
1 (4-inch) cinnamon stick
8 whole cloves

1. Place the oranges in a large, heatproof glass or ceramic bowl or a glass or ceramic baking dish in which they'll fit in a single layer; set aside.

2. In a small, heavy saucepan over medium heat, bring the water and sugar to a boil, stirring to dissolve the sugar. Simmer until the mixture is slightly thickened (it will start to look dense, more like syrup than water), 8 to 10 minutes. Immediately pour the liquid over the oranges and let cool to room temperature.

3. When the oranges have cooled, lift them from the liquid and place them in individual serving bowls. Return the liquid to the saucepan, add the cinnamon stick and cloves, and bring to a boil over medium heat. Lower the heat and simmer until the liquid is reduced by half, 5 to 8 minutes. Remove and discard the spices and pour the syrup over the oranges.

SERVES 8

2/Chocolate Espresso Bourbon Cake

The basic recipe for this cake (which includes a pound of chocolate and one whole tablespoon of flour) gets passed around from cook to cook because it is so good and so easy. I felt like a genius the first time I made it (right after I got over the shock that it only takes fifteen minutes to bake). As convenient and speedy as that seems, the cake does require foresight: Make it the day before (or at least the morning of) the day you plan on serving it. Refrigeration gives the cake a truffle-like texture.

Serving Options

➤ On a plate, all by itself: bare-naked chocolate cake that tastes like bourbon. Nothing wrong with that.

➤ Plated with whipped cream or ice cream (the cake is already rich with hints of bourbon and espresso, so keep the flavors basic)

➤ With chocolate sauce and raspberries

➤ With chocolate sauce and segments of poached oranges (no kidding: Chocolate and orange is a fab flavor combo)

➤ Cut into small pieces and served like brownies alongside *dulce de leche* ice cream, or added to a cookie plate (page 160).

THE EQUIPMENT: SPRINGFORM PAN, METAL COOLING RACK
A springform is a round metal baking pan with a removable bottom and high, straight sides. A latch on the outside snaps open so you can remove the pan from a delicate cake rather than struggling to extract the cake from the pan. Springforms come in several sizes. For the Chocolate Espresso Bourbon Cake you will need an 8-inch pan.

A footed metal cooling rack (look for closely spaced grids) will hold a baking pan or cookie sheet up and off the counter, preventing condensation, allowing air to circulate freely, and reducing cooling time.

CHOCOLATE ESPRESSO BOURBON CAKE

1 lb. superior-quality semi- or bittersweet chocolate, broken into squares or coarsely chopped
1 tablespoon instant espresso granules
⅛ teaspoon ground cinnamon
10 tablespoons unsalted butter, cut into small pieces while cold and brought to room temperature
1 tablespoon granulated sugar
1 tablespoon unbleached all-purpose flour
Pinch of coarse or kosher salt
4 large eggs, separated
2 tablespoons bourbon

1. Preheat the oven to 425°F. Place the rack in the middle of the oven. Line the bottom of an 8-inch springform pan with a round of cooking parchment (see page 30) cut to fit. Lightly spray the parchment and the sides of the pan with nonstick cooking spray; wipe out the excess with a paper towel.

2. In a double boiler suspended over hot (not simmering) water, melt the chocolate with the espresso granules and cinnamon, stirring occasionally, until the chocolate is smooth. Remove the top pan from the double boiler and fold the butter, bit by bit, into the chocolate. Blend in the sugar, flour, and salt. Lightly beat the egg yolks and fold them into the batter.

3. Using an electric mixer, beat the egg whites on medium-high speed until stiff peaks form (when you turn off the mixer and lift the beater out of the bowl, the egg whites should form peaks that hold their shape). Using a rubber spatula, fold half of the egg whites into the chocolate mixture to lighten it (there may still be white streaks in the chocolate). Gently fold in the remaining egg whites, using an over-and-under motion until the batter is smoothly blended and no white streaks remain.

4. Pour the batter into the pan and bake on for exactly 15 minutes (the cake will still be soft, almost runny). Place the pan on a cooling rack and pour the bourbon all over the top of the cake.

5. When the cake is cool, remove the sides of the pan, wrap the cake in plastic wrap, and refrigerate until cold and firm. To serve, invert the cake onto a plate, remove the bottom of the pan, and peel away the parchment. Cut into wedges (8 to 12) or bite-size brownies. Note that cutting this round cake into square or diamond-shaped brownies will leave lots of oddly-shaped little pieces. They're all yours.

THE SKILLS: SEPARATING EGGS
You need to separate eggs to make this cake, so get yourself a cheap egg separator (a one-piece plastic or metal gadget that catches the yolk and lets the white run off). Or use your fingers for the same purpose: Trickier but doable. Break the eggs one at a time into a cup before putting them in the bowl. If you break a yolk, dump that egg and start over. If there's any yolk mixed in with the whites, you won't get much volume when you beat them.

3/Fruit Crisp

If anyone asks, a cobbler is a baked fruit dish with a top crust made from sweetened biscuit dough. A fruit crisp, on the other hand, has a crumbly, streusel-like topping (usually made from flour, sugar, and butter; this version also has nuts). Now, which do you think is easier? There is no reason—absolutely none—that exempts you from being able to make a crisp. If you don't have a food processor, the ingredients for the topping can be placed in a large bowl and rubbed between your fingers until the warmth of your skin softens the butter and a lumpy paste begins to form. Fruit crisps are a mainstay American dessert, and although dunce-cap easy, they deliver a simple but stunning dessert statement: "Yes, I made it myself."

If there's any secret, it is to pick fresh, ripe (but still slightly firm) fruit that provides true flavor. If the fruit didn't taste good going into the oven, it won't taste good coming out.

Stacking Textures/ Serving Options

➤ For cold-weather crisps (like pear and apple), serve warm from the oven with whipped cream or ice cream, changing the flavorings to suit the fruit.

➤ Serve cold apple or pear crisps with warm butterscotch sauce and whipped cream.

➤ For summer crisps, like plum or peach, serve cold, with whipped cream or ice cream, changing the flavorings to flatter the filling.

➤ Serve plum or peach crisp warm from the oven for a summer weekend breakfast.

USE EVERYTHING

Be inventive: Use golden raisins and sun-dried cherries or cranberries for the apple crisp; apricots and figs (cut into small pieces) for the pear; sun-dried blueberries for the plum crisp; and sun-dried strawberries mixed with golden raisins for the peach. Match the flavoring to the fruit: Try Calvados for apple crisp, cassis for plum, dark rum for pear, and bourbon or Frangelico for peach.

FRUIT CRISP

FOR THE TOPPING

½ cup unbleached all-purpose flour
½ cup firmly packed light brown sugar
½ cup shelled walnuts
5 tablespoons unsalted butter, chilled

FOR THE FILLING

⅓ cup dried fruit
1 tablespoon liquor, nut or fruit liqueur or brandy
4½ cups fresh fruit (pears, peaches, apples, or plums), unpeeled, in small (about ½-inch) dice
2 tablespoons lemon juice
1 teaspoon vanilla extract
1 tablespoon unbleached all-purpose flour
1 tablespoon granulated sugar
Pinch of ground nutmeg
Pinch of ground cinnamon
Pinch of ground allspice

1. Place the flour, sugar, and walnuts in a food processor and process until combined (use quick pulses; the nuts should not be ground). Cut the butter into small pieces and add to the food processor, pulsing until a lumpy paste is formed (about 30 seconds). Refrigerate until ready to use.

2. Place the dried fruit in a small heatproof bowl and cover with boiling water. Set aside until the fruit softens and plumps, about 30 minutes. Drain the water and toss the fruit with the liquor, liqueur or brandy.

3. Place the fresh fruit in a large mixing bowl, sprinkle with lemon juice, and toss. Add the vanilla and toss again. Sprinkle in the dried fruit with its liquid and toss to evenly distribute. Sprinkle the flour, sugar, and spices over the fruit and toss to coat. Let the fruit mixture stand at room temperature (to draw out natural juices) for at least 30 minutes.

4. Preheat the oven to 400°F. Place the rack in the upper third of the oven

5. Spoon the fruit into a 9 x 9-inch ovenproof glass baking dish. Crumble the cold topping over the fruit and bake until the topping is crisp and browned and the fruit is bubbling around the edges, about 30 minutes. If serving warm, cool on a wire rack for about 10 minutes. If serving cold, cool to room temperature, then cover with plastic wrap and refrigerate.

SERVES 4

The Best Fruit

The flavor and sweetness of fruit vary from tart to bland to stupendous, depending on the season and variety.

Taste the apples, pears, peaches, or plums before you start, and adjust the amounts of dried fruit, sugar, spices, and other seasonings to boost the overall flavor, sweetness, or tartness as needed. (Be warned, though, there is no such thing as "adding less.") To serve 8, double the recipe and use a 13 x 9-inch ovenproof glass baking dish.

4/Cookie Plate

Without getting all Proustian, I think it is safe to say that cookies have a retro, Real McCoy appeal, and that baking them conjures up all sorts of images about home and hearth and simple pleasures—images that marketing departments are only too happy to exploit. I've noticed that on those frozen cookie dough commercials, the mom is often wearing an apron as she slices the roll of storebought dough into rounds and transfers them to a pan. What's the apron for? Where's the floury mess in that? But commercialization doesn't change the fact that cookies are charming desserts for home entertaining (alone, or alongside poached oranges, fruit crisps, or ice cream): proof positive that not only has someone been in the kitchen—someone cares about what comes out.

Serving Options
- ➤ Purist: one type of cookie
- ➤ Classicist: two types of cookies
- ➤ Realist: three types of cookies
- ➤ Extremist: all three cookies plus Chocolate Espresso Bourbon Cake cut into bite-sized brownies.

THE EQUIPMENT: OVEN THERMOMETER
Baking isn't the same as cooking—it's more precise, like chemistry. If you want to be good at it, you have to follow the recipe and use the right equipment. To guarantee accurate baking temperatures, use a stainless steel, spring-action oven thermometer that stands on or hangs from the oven rack. The spring expands as the oven heats up and moves the pointer on the face of the dial. Place the thermometer on the rack in the center of the oven and preheat the oven (at the temperature specified in the recipe) for at least twenty minutes. Then adjust the oven temperature control, if necessary, until the thermometer says you've got it right.

LEMON SHORTBREAD

I don't know who first tried using a fine rasp from the hardware store to grate lemon zest, but it worked so well that microplanes are now standard equipment in every kitchen supply store.

> 1 cup (2 sticks) unsalted butter, at room temperature
> ½ cup granulated sugar, plus 1 tablespoon for sprinkling
> Pinch of coarse or kosher salt
> 1 teaspoon vanilla extract
> 2 tablespoons minced lemon zest
> 2 cups unbleached all-purpose flour

1. Preheat the oven to 325°F. Lightly coat a strip tart pan with nonstick cooking spray, wiping out the excess with a paper towel.

2. Using an electric mixer, beat the butter, ½ cup of the sugar, and the salt on medium speed until fluffy. Stir in the vanilla and lemon zest. Gradually add the flour about ½ cup at a time, beating on low speed after each addition.

3. Scraping the sides and bottom of the bowl, gather the dough together and place it in the tart pan. Press the dough gently and evenly into the pan, making sure the corners are filled, then lightly sprinkle the surface with the remaining 1 tablespoon sugar. Using the tines of a fork, prick the surface of the dough in evenly spaced rows: 9 down the length and 4 across the width.

4. Bake until the shortbread is a pale golden color and the corners are just starting to turn brown, 40 to 45 minutes. Do not overbake: Your fingers should leave a slight indentation when you press down lightly on the shortbread. While the shortbread is still hot, cut between the "dotted lines" to make 18 squares. Place the pan on a wire rack and remove the shortbreads only when completely cool.

MAKES 18 BAR COOKIES

THE EQUIPMENT: TART PAN
A strip tart pan is a rectangular (about 14 x 4 inches) metal pan with fluted sides and a removable bottom.

PEANUT BUTTER AND CHOCOLATE KISS COOKIES

Unwrap the chocolate kisses carefully so the tips of the curlicue peaks survive intact.

1¾ cups unbleached all-purpose flour
½ teaspoon baking powder
½ teaspoon baking soda
½ cup (1 stick) unsalted butter, at room temperature
½ cup crunchy peanut butter
¾ cup firmly packed light brown sugar
¼ cup granulated sugar
1 large egg, at room temperature
1 teaspoon vanilla
Milk chocolate kisses (at least 36), unwrapped

1. Preheat the oven to 350°F. Line several sheet pans with cooking parchment or use a Silpat liner (see page 30).

2. In a bowl, combine the flour, baking powder, and baking soda, and stir well; set aside.

3. In a large mixing bowl, using an electric mixer, beat the butter, peanut butter, and brown and granulated sugars on low speed until fluffy. Add the egg and beat until well combined. Stir in the vanilla. Gradually add the flour mixture, ½ cup at a time, beating on low speed until thoroughly blended.

4. Shape the dough into walnut-size balls. Place 2 inches apart on the prepared pans. Bake until light golden (the cookies will still be soft), 8 to 10 minutes.

5. Remove the pan from the oven and immediately place a chocolate kiss in the center of each cookie, pressing down gently but firmly. Transfer the cookies to a rack to cool completely.

MAKES ABOUT 36 COOKIES

THE SKILLS: HOW TO ROLL OUT AND CUT COOKIE DOUGH

Let the chilled dough sit at room temperature until it is the right consistency for rolling and cutting (pliable but not soft and sticky). Now you will encounter "The Problem:" Dusting the rolling surface with flour keeps the dough from sticking and tearing, but too much flour makes the dough tough. The solution: Use a Silpat mat (see page 30) as a rolling surface. Buy the full sheet-pan size (24½ x 16½ inches). The nonstick surface minimizes the need for additional flour. If your cookie cutter begins to stick, dip it in flour or confectioner's (powdered) sugar. As for rolling pins, a little practice with a tapered one-piece European-style pin and you'll never use the standard American pin (with handles) again.

GINGER SPICE COOKIES

This recipe calls for a plain or fluted round cookie cutter. You will discover that cookie cutters are available in more whimsical shapes (such as planes, trains, and automobiles). Just remember that the more ornate the shape of the cutter, the greater the chance that the cookie will crack or break.

3¾ **cups unbleached all-purpose flour**
¼ **cup unsweetened cocoa powder (Hershey's is fine)**
2 **tablespoons pumpkin-pie spice**
1½ **teaspoons ground cloves**
¾ **teaspoon baking soda**
Pinch of coarse or kosher salt
1 **cup (2 sticks) unsalted butter, at room temperature**
1 **cup granulated sugar**
1 **large egg, at room temperature**
½ **cup unsulfured molasses**

1. Preheat the oven to 350°F. Line several sheet pans with cooking parchment or use a Silpat liner (see page 30).

2. In a medium bowl, combine the flour, cocoa, spices, baking soda, and salt, and stir well; set aside.

3. In a large mixing bowl, using an electric mixer, beat the butter and sugar together at medium speed until fluffy. Beat in the egg until the mixture is a bright golden color, then beat in the molasses. Gradually add the flour mixture, ½ cup at a time, beating on low speed until well combined.

4. Gather the dough into a ball, divide it in half, and pat each portion of dough into a thick disk. Wrap the dough in plastic wrap and refrigerate until the dough is easy to work with, about 90 minutes.

5. On a lightly floured surface, roll out the dough about ½ inch thick. Using a plain or fluted circular cutter about 2 inches in diameter, cut out cookies and place them on the prepared pans. Bake, rotating the pans once, until the edges of the cookies begin to brown, 10 to 12 minutes. Let the cookies cool on the pans for several minutes before using a small offset spatula (see page 95) to transfer them to a rack to cool. Store in an airtight container.

MAKES ABOUT 40 COOKIES

THE EQUIPMENT: MEASURING CUPS AND SPOONS

For successful baking you need to measure carefully and correctly. Cups for measuring dry ingredients cups come in nested sets (¼, ⅓, ½ and 1 cup); the best are stainless steel. The most useful liquid measuring cups are made of ovenproof glass, with bright red markings up the side (the 2-cup size is most practical). Standard measuring spoons come in a set of five (⅛, ¼, ½ and 1 teaspoon, and 1 tablespoon). For small amounts of liquid, I use a shot glass that's marked off in tablespoons and ounces.

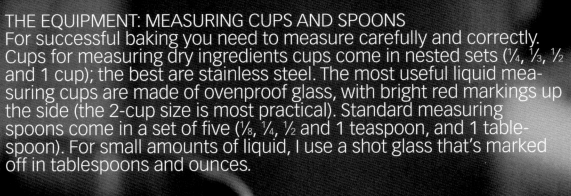

For starters, be sure you
buy heavy cream (some-
times labeled heavy whip-
ping cream); light cream,
coffee cream, half & half,
and other permutations
won't work. The cream
needs to be icy cold, or
you'll never get where
you're going, so chill the
beaters and bowl (a small,
deep one), as well as the
cream, in the refrigerator
for at least two hours
before whipping time. You
want to add sweeteners, if
any, toward the end of the
whipping process; sweet-
ened cream takes longer
to whip.

5/Over the Top/Whipped Cream and Dessert Sauces

Whipped cream—plain or flavored—and dessert sauces not only
enhance the flavor, texture, and color of whatever you may be serving;
they also double as the best kind of plate decoration: edible.

WHIPPED CREAM

*Freshly whipped cream is enough of a treat, even unsweetened. Boosting the oomph
depends on what you're serving* under *the whipped cream. Add flavorings and sweeteners sparingly, using the measurements given in the recipe as a baseline. Then make
adjustments after performing this two-step taste test: (1) Stick finger in whipped cream.
(2) Stick said finger in mouth.*

1 cup heavy cream, well chilled

Mix-and-match flavorings to taste:
2 teaspoons brown sugar
1 teaspoon vanilla extract
2 teaspoons bourbon, dark or coconut rum, or Kahlúa
½ teaspoon instant coffee
Pinch of ground cinnamon, cloves, or nutmeg (go easy on the spices)

1. Pour the cream into a deep, well-chilled mixing bowl. Using a hand-
held mixer on low speed, beat the cream, gradually increasing the speed to
high as the cream thickens (if you start out on high speed, the cream will
splatter).

2. When the cream is thick enough to form soft peaks (it should not have
the stiff consistency of the stuff that comes out of an aerosol nozzle), add sugar
and flavorings (sweetened cream takes longer to whip) and beat until combined. The cream will double in volume.

165

Make dessert sauces before your guests arrive, then reheat gently at serving time. Sometimes I heat the sauce in a double boiler suspended over simmering water. It takes longer, but it also holds the sauce without over-boiling and scorching it. And I can focus on other things because I don't have to worry about it.

BUTTERSCOTCH SAUCE

Perfect for any dessert that isn't chocolate: Think pumpkin pudding, apple crisp, warm gingerbread, or vanilla ice cream.

¼ **cup unsalted butter**
½ **cup firmly packed light brown sugar**
½ **cup granulated sugar**
½ **cup light corn syrup**
1 cup heavy cream
1 tablespoon vanilla extract (or dark rum or bourbon)
1 tablespoon lemon juice

1. In a small, heavy saucepan melt the butter and the brown and granulated sugars over low heat. Stir in the corn syrup. Whisk in the cream, increase the heat to medium, and bring the mixture to a short, gentle boil. Reduce the heat and simmer gently, stirring occasionally, until the sauce is thickened, 12 to 15 minutes. (Beware: The simmering mixture may splatter, and it will hurt.)

2. Remove the pan from the heat and pour the sauce into a heatproof storage container. Stir in the vanilla and lemon juice. When cooled, cover and refrigerate until ready to use.

MAKES 2 CUPS

CHOCOLATE SAUCE

This velvety sauce makes so many simple desserts as rich as you wanna be: Think coffee ice cream, Chocolate Espresso Bourbon Cake with raspberries, or warm pecan pie.

12 tablespoons (1½ sticks) unsalted butter
8 ounces bittersweet chocolate, coarsely chopped
½ cup granulated sugar
⅓ cup light corn syrup
1 cup heavy cream
1 teaspoon vanilla extract
2 teaspoons bourbon

1. In a small, heavy saucepan melt the butter and chocolate over low heat, stirring frequently. Stir in the sugar, then add the corn syrup. Slowly whisk in the cream and bring to a gentle boil. Immediately reduce the heat and simmer the sauce gently until thickened, about 5 minutes. Stir frequently, scraping down the sides of the saucepan with a rubber spatula.

2. Remove the pan from the heat and pour the sauce into a heatproof storage container. Stir in the vanilla and bourbon. When the sauce is cool, cover and refrigerate until ready to use.

MAKES 2 CUPS

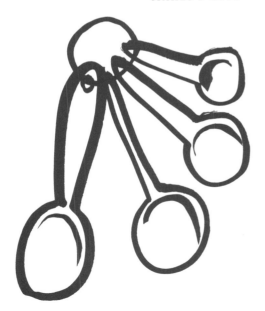

The flavor and texture of different kinds of chocolate are determined by complicated proportions of chocolate liquor (not a beverage, but the essence of roasted cocoa beans) to other ingredients. But generally speaking:

• Dark chocolate (like bittersweet and semisweet) is heavy on the chocolate liquor and light on the sugar, which gives it a rich, intense taste. If you are sampling, always taste dark chocolate last..

• Milk chocolate has less chocolate liquor and more sugar, plus milk or cream, which makes it milder and sweeter.

• White chocolate has no chocolate liquor at all: just cocoa butter (in high-quality brands), sugar, milk, and vanilla. The flavor is very sweet and delicate. Cheap white "chocolate" bears no resemblance at all to real chocolate: Don't buy it, don't serve it, don't eat it.

6/Behold, the Power of Chocolate . . . Truffles

In the 1982 film *E.T.,* Elliot may have been a strange little loner of a kid, but he was clever enough to know that with the right candy, you can lure anyone anywhere. I have followed Elliot's lead myself, serving all kinds of tempting sweets—from cold peanut butter cups to chocolate-covered cherries—after dinner, to tempt a guest away from the table and over to the couch. But if your intention is to take that trip one step further, you're going to have to get your hands on some truffles.

Chocolate truffles are named after the other truffles—edible fungi that grow around certain trees—mostly because they are similarly shaped and colored (and almost as costly). For people like me, who live in cities where chocolate truffles are still being made by hand, finding the best is a pleasurable process. For those who live in less truffle-intensive parts of the county, finding *any* seems to the problem.

After much tasting here and there, I have settled on getting my truffles from El Eden—an 11 x 21-foot jewel box in New York's East Village where detail-conscious craftsmanship and service shine. If that's too long a trip to take (even for truffles), here are some shopping tips from Wai Chu, the chocolatier (and, along with partner Marjorie Dybec, co-owner of El Eden).

The Best Truffles

First, Chu says, it is important to understand that there are subjective and objective criteria in evaluating chocolate, and it is a combination of these factors that creates the identity of the truffle. Here's what to look for:

Objective Criteria:

➤ **Appearance: overall sheen.** The surface of the truffle should look good, with even coloration (no cloudy, whitish streaks or dots).

➤ **Aroma: deep and flavorful.** You may not be able to detect the individual flavoring through the shell of the truffle, but the chocolate itself should smell fresh: "real" and not artificial. "It should open up," says Wai, "like wine that breathes."

➤ **Mouth-feel: a snap followed by silkiness.** When you take the first bite, the chocolate shell should make a delicate crack and break cleanly, without crumbling. When the ganache (the interior of the truffle, a blend of chocolate and cream) hits the roof of your mouth, you want velvety, smooth, and creamy (not greasy or gummy). And again, the flavor should have length, like wine (it shouldn't just "pop" and be gone).

Subjective Criteria

➤ **The size.** This is a matter of personal taste—yours and the chocolatier's. "We make ours for two healthy bites," says Wai, "so you can enjoy the richness of the truffle. Oversized is too big a mouthful; too small may be disappointing."

➤ **The coating.** The outer design of a truffle often reflects the flavor of the ganache (for example, the crème brûlée truffle, with its vanilla- and caramel-flavored core, is covered in white chocolate and caramel crystals). "When we flavor with liqueur, we take care to add just enough to enhance the flavor of the ganache, not overpower it. For example, the dark chocolate and orange essence has just a hint of Benedictine."

➤ **The shopping experience itself.** No matter how intricate the design, chocolate truffles should still look and smell like food, and not "gifts." (In my case, I never buy chocolate in a store that also sells potpourri or scented candles; just a quirk I've developed over the years.) Nor should you feel intimated, as though the counter were a barricade. The sales help should do just that, helping you to decide upon an assortment and offering samples (limited, of course).

Acknowledgments

It doesn't take a genius to figure out that you don't write a book entitled *Esquire Eats* without *Esquire*, and I thank Editor-in-Chief David Granger and Brendan Vaughan for their time, trouble, and faith that the *Esquire* attitude can reside north of the waist. I would also like to thank Betty Rice who shaped the concept for this book, and Lee Fowler and Bonnie Slotnick who guided it to completion.

It's hard to get a writer-in-residence gig for a cookbook, and I am grateful to the following friends who turned their homes into stress-free recipe testing zones: Justin Spring and Tony Korner, Suzanne and Peter Pollak, and, in Philadelphia, Chez Mitchell Gruner, where Paul Curci, Wayne Aretz, Ellen Yin, and Kevin Hills came over and ate whatever I made no matter how hot it was during that July Fourth weekend.

I take special pleasure in thanking my agent, Laura Blake Peterson, and her assistant, Kelly Going, because it means we're finally done with this one, and express gratitude to all who helped make it possible: Marcia Warner, Jan Fort, Melissa Vaughan, Priscilla Warner, Randy Neff, Andrew French, Jay Woodruff, Steve Brown, Anthony Gentile, George Proschnick, Wendy Israel, Wayne Gryk, Maryanne Bannon, Kevin McDonnell, and Celia Fuller. I am also grateful to the late Lee Bailey for everything he taught me.

Most of all, I would like to thank my father, Marty, and my mother, Maddie, who is here even when she isn't.

Francine Maroukian
New York City

Index